SURRENDER

SURRENDER

FEMINIST RHETORIC AND ETHICS IN LOVE AND ILLNESS

JESSICA RESTAINO

Southern Illinois University Press
Carbondale

Southern Illinois University Press
www.siupress.com

22 21 20 19   4 3 2 1

Cover illustration: Wendy Osterweil, *Filomena and Rosa*,
2014, silkscreen printed with fiber reactive dyes on
viscose rayon, 4 feet × 8 feet, Philadelphia.

Library of Congress Cataloging-in-Publication Data
Names: Restaino, Jessica, 1976– author.
Title: Surrender : feminist rhetoric and ethics in love and illness
/ Jessica Restaino.
Description: Carbondale : Southern Illinois University Press, [2019] |
Includes bibliographical references and index.
Identifiers: LCCN 2018022962 | ISBN 9780809337149 (paperback) |
ISBN 9780809337156 (e-book)
Subjects: LCSH: Academic writing—Social aspects. |
Rhetoric—Social aspects. | Feminist theory.
Classification: LCC P301.5.A27 R47 2019 | DDC 808.02—dc23
LC record available at https://lccn.loc.gov/2018022962

For Sue

I am knowing
All about
        Unfolding

—Mina Loy, "Parturition," 1914

CONTENTS

ACKNOWLEDGMENTS

This book emerges from a period in my life filled with great loss and also great growth. I think there is no other book I could have written at this moment, and I hope this work—its strengths and shortcomings considered—might serve as a kind of testament to the ways in which hardship and loss can also be generative. Struggle can indeed bind us together and birth possibility. Every page here is wrought of many relationships that have helped me along, shown me new pathways, inspired and moved me.

Numerous talented, smart readers provided insights into this manuscript as I worked. I want to thank first the blind reviewers for Southern Illinois University Press, whose open, engaged, and honest reading inspired and guided me through the last revisions. Kristine Priddy at SIU Press is a visionary and brave editor, and it's been my honor to work with her again. I am grateful to the many friends who read drafts for me, talked and listened, and offered invaluable direction. Stephanie Kerschbaum, Paula Mathieu, Jay Dolmage, and Sondra Perl each read chapters or drafts of conference presentations that would turn into chapters. Caroline Dadas and Lisa Blankenship listened thoughtfully and compassionately and shared smart insights as I rehearsed my first talk on this work following Sue's death; their friendship is a gift. My thanks go to Rachel Gramer for her friendship and for her valuable work on narrativity; our conversations have taught me so much. Jenn Fishman is a brilliant thinking partner, and our regular video chats are a buoy to my brain and also to my need to laugh. Special thanks go to Jenn, too, and Jessica Enoch for their insightful reading and risk-taking as coeditors of the special issue of *Peitho*, where excerpts of this longer work first appeared. I am grateful to the Coalition of Feminist Scholars in the History of Rhetoric and Composition for featuring my "reverse interview" workshop, inspired by my work with Sue, as part of the "Action Hour" at the 2016 Conference on College Composition and Communication and for including a digital publication of this workshop in the "Performing Feminist Action" toolkit on the Coalition's website. Eli Goldblatt, one of my most enduring teachers, read a draft and held many long conversations with me about this work and all the rest of life. Eli's ability to envision the thing when my words are inarticulate or partial has been for many years a source of faith for me. I treasure Lisa Ede's deep reserves of intellect and care, and this work has benefited tremendously from her careful reading of both early and late sections. Lisa's friendship and mentoring have been a light on the road of grief, healing, and writing.

There are yet others who have driven me forward and through this book with unique generosities. My thanks go to Jessica Benjamin for her brave work, for her responsiveness to my questions, and for pointing me in the direction of her six-part essay, "The Discarded and the Dignified," from which I learned so much. Thanks also go to Jacqueline Rhodes for sharing her 2016 CCCC paper with me and for being a bold voice. The support and professionalism of my colleagues (and sisterhood) in the writing program at Montclair, especially Jennifer Holly-Wells, Laura Field, Bonnie Dowd, and Caroline Dadas, helped me to carve out the time and energy to write. Kurt Maute, my permanent friend, has been an enduring, supportive presence as we have each traveled along. Rosemarie Ciccarello's extraordinary combination of intellect, skill, and heart made it possible for me to write this book at all; my many references to "making space" are an homage to her teaching. My very best friend and my partner in the throes of life, Ryan Kline, has been and continues to be a believer who routinely dusts me off and picks me up. Our daughters, Abby and Thalia Kline, inspire me every day with their radical growth.

And of course, finally and fully: my deepest gratitude to my friend Susan Lundy Maute, who showed me what it means to be brave.

SURRENDER

A NECESSARY SCAN
BEAUTIFUL MESS, DARK ENERGY
THIS BOOK

> And thank you for being eyes [when] I cannot see for myself.
> —*Susan Lundy Maute to Jessica Restaino,*
> *9 July 2014 correspondence*

This book is a coming together of darkness and light, a torqued methodology. It employs both social scientific and humanistic methods for research while giving in fully to neither. It is a book about how and why we write as academics but also how and why we write as persons whose relationship to language is desperately intimate and frustratingly inadequate. Taking its lessons from the edges of terminal illness, friendship, the failing body, the need for human connectedness, and an urgency to put words to experience, this book testifies to its own impossibilities. It is an enactment of the shortcomings of our ability to understand, mixed helplessly with a dogged faith in language to deliver us closer. This book acknowledges its cancer.

Beautiful Mess

We were hiking a familiar trail in the woods when my friend Susan Lundy Maute turned to me and said, "Ask me whatever you want. I'm an open book." I faltered. As if adjusting binoculars to get a clearer picture, I felt myself alternatingly leaning in and back. Sue's situation was serious: stage IV breast cancer, now permanently on her bone. And her persona was complex: strong, private, tough, smart. I did not think she was an open book, but I also felt the pull of our connection and what

1

I sensed, potentially, as a need in her to share her experience of living with breast cancer. Weeks later she would visit the class I was teaching, Rhetoric of Sport, to talk about her own exceptional athleticism in relation to her terminal status. In class, students and I explored athletes' rhetorical constructions of physical prowess, competition, triumph, and failure. We wondered together: In what ways are athletes—and the feats of their bodies—built in words? Soon we moved from celebrities to nontraditional athletes, octogenarian sprinters, and amputee marathoners. How do these athletes construct alternate meanings around the value of athleticism, physical accomplishment, and competition? What is the role of language in enacting such physical accomplishment and this unique orientation to the limits of the body? As we wrestled with these questions, Sue quickly became someone I wanted to invite into our classroom conversation. She had won a national championship playing collegiate field hockey and, despite living with breast cancer, continued to compete years later. How did she construct meaning in this use of her body? How did she understand, rhetorically, the experience of pushing her physical limits athletically while living with terminal cancer?

Ultimately, those first questions and that first invitation opened a collaboration between Sue and me, a project of writing and talking our way through terminal illness, that would last the remaining two years of her life. We did not know when we started that her disease would soon begin its movement from bone to soft tissue, from manageable to destructive. But by the time of this shift, we were intellectually and emotionally entwined, bound by a process of writing, reading, and talking that rendered us journey partners to the end of her life. I'll offer further context for our collaboration in the following pages, and of course the dynamics of our relationship will continue to unfold over the whole of this book. But here I want to capture a transitional moment. A little over a year into our collaboration, Sue and I copresented at the 2013 Feminisms and Rhetorics Conference, which was held at Stanford University that year (Sue joined us via video conference from the East Coast). At that time, the transition of the cancer from bone to tissue had only recently taken place, and treatment continued to keep the small growth on her liver at bay. Still, there was much uncertainty, and so our presentation explored the changing nature of our collaboration, our movement into an increasingly unpredictable process and less-defined roles. We held this sense of uncertainty between us in ways that at once pulled us closer while also emphasizing our very different standpoints, exposing who we each were in relation to, and as distinct from, the other. At the time, I described my "researcher" role in the context of Marjorie DeVault's call for "involvement as an element of method" and began what would be a deepening process, complicating my own experience of "the personal" in my relationship to my work:

> In many ways, surrendering to this project, to the slipperiness of my role, has equally emphasized our respective distance and highlighted our respective "personal," our relative standpoints. In the quiet, I am okay with that—just as Sue writes "I'm okay with being alone and it feels right." Reflecting on DeVault . . . , I must ask: where is the line between "experience" and "method"? What is lost when we "discipline" the personal? Is such a disciplining even possible? If so, what might be gained? How far have I surrendered? How much further will I go? These are questions I ask while I wonder if answers—any answers—are even within reach. (Restaino and Maute, "No Evidence" 16)

There was an inevitable "aloneness" to our collaboration: this, on one hand, felt a lot like being along together, on an island of sorts with the experience of Sue's evolving disease, her shifting perspective on her changing body, her orienting and then reorienting to time itself. These were things we held between us, that we talked and wrote about in ways that united us deeply. But the questions I pose here—especially "How much further will I go?"—speak directly to our distance, to the fact that only one of us had, in a sense, no choice in road. This status marked Sue's unique isolation. I could, I suppose, have ducked out, faded away, or dashed in fear as the impending swell of the disease loomed, drawing this distance still further.

But something happened, something tremendous, at that conference. Maybe it was the experience of being the sole "terminal" representative on a conference panel dedicated to breast cancer, listening to the other two presenters who could carry the title "survivor" when she could not, or maybe it was the silent, growing current of her disease that would, in the coming weeks, begin to make her deeply ill: Sue fell uncharacteristically to pieces after our presentation. We got on the phone following our panel to debrief, talk about how things went, discuss the other presentations. She shared her frustration at her own denied "survivorship," a common chasm between stage IV cancer patients and those who've undergone treatment and demonstrate "no evidence of disease." She felt misled by the assurances she had received earlier in her treatment, that this would be an "open and shut" case, that she had a "good" kind of breast cancer. Having made the decision not to get breast implants, she expressed her disappointment at depictions of "sexy" breast surgery following cancer treatment, a common trope in popular representations of breast cancer survivorship.[1] Our fellow panelists touched on all of these topics, unintentionally deepening Sue's wounds. But most painfully, she told me a story about a recent argument with one of her daughters, who had been insisting she no longer wanted to play on the high school field hockey team. Hoping for her daughter to have the same support and camaraderie she had experienced as an athlete, Sue had blurted out: "Listen, I may not always be here . . ." This was a startling, first acknowledgment of the severity of her disease to one of her children and, for Sue, a great betrayal of her devotion to protecting her kids from what was the frightening, threatening reality of her illness. It all came gushing out.

Despite our physical locations on opposite ends of the country, this conversation pulled us perhaps closer than ever before. Listening to her words as they tumbled forward, listening to her weeping, I had, of course, nothing "right" or useful to say. I could feel my heart pushing its way helplessly toward her voice. As she followed up with the qualification, "I mean, I want to see them through, you know, and I told her it's my goal to see you through . . ." I heard myself saying, "I know. I know you do. I know it is." And then she told me about what would be, ultimately, one of her last truly free moments of sport, of celebrating her own vast athleticism. I wrote this story out, reflecting on our conversation after we hung up the phone, and so I quote my own record at length here:

> She described having a great "run"—dodging easily through three players at the top of the circle. She said . . . *you know how it is when you don't really mean to do it . . . but it just comes together perfectly?* I did know. And she said . . . *and then I pulled the ball to my left and just did a reverse drive. I thought either I'm going to totally miss or I'm going to connect.* And she connected and she scored. And it was beautiful—a perfect goal. And then Sue explained to me—that she found herself, just after this moment, tearing up, becoming overwhelmed with emotion as she acknowledged that there may be a time soon when she can't do that any more. The feeling of loss—or impending loss—came ushered in by great joy. ("Notes on Sue's Goal")

While we did not know it then, she had under a year to live at the time of the Feminisms and Rhetorics Conference. What I did know then and in that moment, on the phone, listening with nothing to say and yet understanding in body, as an athlete myself, what she described, was this: I would walk it the whole way if she wanted me to. I do not know why this was so, did not understand it then or really now, nor was I free of fear. But I felt with great clarity my role to walk alongside, as witness, as keeper of her private grief. It would be that grief and loss she wanted so desperately to spare her children, her family, that would find its place securely between us, held and kept and nurtured in talk and writing until she was gone. In reality she would not, could not, spare her family the pain, of course. In some ways I think she took refuge from that awareness in the private space between us. It feels obvious to say there is of course something very certain about death. But to follow language through the process of coming to terms with death and through the hope that someone else—in this case, me—could understand something about what that coming to terms feels like is a shared, intimate rhetoric. It is also always somewhat unstable and uncertain, and perhaps this is in part because it must happen between us, a back and forth, jumbled and messy, always limited by what separates us and yet always driven by our desire to understand and be understood.

In this collaborative, intimate pact of sorts, Sue and I generated a large body of text: written correspondence, interview transcripts, informal writings that we each did at certain critical points, collaborative texts we worked on together. In her way, Sue gave all of this over to me fully. I sit now alone, without my friend and collaborator, among all of these rhetorical artifacts, many of them deeply personal. This introduces into the book a host of ethical considerations with which I expect I'll continue to struggle even long after publication. We went through a series of conversations around this material, though none were ever quite satisfyingly conclusive. While Sue was still alive, I worked on an essay for a special issue of the journal *Peitho*.[2] I sought out my university's Institutional Review Board, expecting all sorts of complications given Sue's status as terminally ill. I was advised, however, that if I considered her even a "verbal coauthor," there was no reason to pursue a formal review process for research with human subjects. And so I didn't; I was so very happy to have her name with mine as coauthor for that essay. But still, as the work of actual composing was mine, I wanted her final approval for how I had assembled the piece, for the choices I made from among her many verbal contributions. We sat across from each other at a diner, and I implored her to please read the first draft. "I trust you," she said, salting her eggs and shrugging off the task. But still I pressed, explaining that it mattered to me that she approved of how I represented her and that even with the best of intentions I could represent her in ways she might find inaccurate. And so Sue read the *Peitho* essay, "Surrender as Method," and I received her feedback via text message: "Read the essay. Very impressive. Found a few typos. Also, you make me sound like a valley girl at one point!" (Maute, "Re: Essay Feedback"). I fixed the typos and cleaned up the "valley girl," and we called it done. To a certain extent she would lean into and out of our work: forward for the process itself, back for the product. She "owned" our relationship and its constant motion, inviting me to go forward with her always, but Sue often disowned the material texts born of our collaboration—she didn't need to review or reread or edit; she just put our many artifacts into my hands. This is an important aspect of our dynamic and one I'll return to throughout the book.

The "Surrender as Method" essay is the seed for this larger book project. My central goal in that essay was to capture the experience of essentially losing touch with a research project, unlearning the process of asking questions and moving through a method. Sue's voice in the essay runs parallel to my own experience, as she describes her process of living with terminal breast cancer as one of letting go, releasing expectations for outcomes, and moving back and forth between the concrete (science, medicine) and the metaphysical. The essay ultimately is meant to open questions about how and why we do our work in feminist rhetorical studies. This book grows from that first essay and extends a cross-disciplinary invitation to scholars whose work might resonate for its contact with human struggle, materiality, and loss. Even as I continue to work out of my field of rhetoric-composition, I cast a wide disciplinary net: exploring theoretical frameworks that make versions of "surrender as method" possible and even necessary, as in the case of my collaboration with Sue; modeling applications for how we might do such work; and challenging expectations for the researcher role. Along the way this book asks us to think about the inherent, transformative potential of our work to blend the personal and the scholarly and to make something new out of each. I seek to invert or disrupt our expectations, to rethink predictability and our tendency to follow a "course" when it comes to how we write and do research. Accordingly, cancer, as embodied through these pages, regresses rather than progresses: the first chapter is named after the most advanced, most threatening stage, "Stage IV," and the last chapter after the least threatening, "In Situ," to connote "ductal carcinoma in situ," considered the most treatable breast cancer diagnosis (thanks, in part, to its status as noninvasive or essentially isolated in the milk ducts). I will outline the content of these chapters shortly. In between each formal chapter, readers will find intertexts, which are raw, primary source materials: personal writing, an interview transcript, text messages. These artifacts are meant to interrupt and also inform the flow of the more formal chapters of the book, which in and of themselves consist of much movement back and forth between analysis and narrative, pulling moments from our lived experience together into conversation with a field. I have named the intertexts between chapters "Bloodworks" to indicate this human flow as well as the experience of "getting bloodwork," a routine process in the life of any cancer patient. My hope is that the reader will feel a living presence as well as an interest in disrupting or reimagining our routines throughout these pages.

Ultimately, this book marks my own effort to stay in work that overwhelms me, that pushes me to confront my own humanity and my capacity for pain and for love as rhetorical work. While certainly this often means that we must make room for hybridized methods and for writing that cuts across or destabilizes our more comfortable notions of academic genre, I am most interested in exploring the ways in which personal and professional transformation is foundational to such projects and thus argue for working "imperfectly," honoring limits as new forms of knowing. For me—and I hope others might find similarly hopeful disciplinary space—such working on the edge is in fact very much within the bounds of feminist rhetorical studies.

As Sue and I followed what was a shared drive to record our conversations and our efforts to think together about her experience of terminal illness, I was aware that we were quickly accumulating enough material for a book, not merely a singular essay. Sue was uniquely, endearingly humble, and so in some ways she communicated her enthusiasm for the idea of a book indirectly. To me she would say that the goal of sharing her own experience was the hope that it "might help someone else," and she mused about how she had always wanted to write a book, even long before we began our collaboration. One sunny July day about a month before her death, she texted me to reaffirm exactly this, adding, "O wise literary one please help poor scatter brained one" (Maute, "Re: O wise literary one"). I had, by then, over our two years of work come to assume the status of ethnographer, keeper of records, the "writer" of our partnership. Her oncologist, cancer counselor, friends, and family all recognized me in this way. My arrival in hospital rooms often meant others would politely make their exit, much to my initial surprise. And so in an effort to be formal, responsible, and thoughtful about what we were clearly doing, I provided Sue with a consent form, despite or in addition to her status as "verbal coauthor," for the sake of laying out the terms of my use of materials for the *Peitho* essay or any longer work that might come of our collaboration. We talked about whether or not anything was "off limits" and also about what she wanted me to do with all the material should that day come—as it did—when she would be gone. I promised her I would destroy anything she wanted destroyed. She shrugged. "What if," I asked, "one of your kids comes to me one day and demands to have all the audio recordings. What would you want me to do?" "I'd want them to know their mother. Just nothing that would hurt anyone," she instructed me.

And though I brought up the topic a few more times, this is as far as she would ever go: an impossible paradox. Such a paradox, however, is one I will embrace throughout this book, as it is at once both methodological and epistemological. We all want to be known and yet not to hurt.[3] We want to control others' perceptions of us, their experiences of us, even as we inherently lack such capacity for control. We also want to control our arguments, our data, our sense of where things fit and where they (we) belong. These are human longings, though we often categorize them as professional. As human beings we ache to be understood in ways we recognize, that show us ourselves through others. While terminal illness involves immersion in powerlessness, it also has the capacity to stir tremendous urgency for recognition, the satisfaction of one's desire to be known.

In turn, I have inherited a contradictory, extraordinary sense of expansive power and powerlessness as a research collaborator and writer. I am the keeper of hours of audio recordings and pages and pages of transcripts, personal writings, and steady correspondence between us. Words and words and words, just winding their way through the last two years of her life, her illness, as they unfolded on our small island, bestowed on me but packaged with slippery directions, boundaries, rules. This now is my great gift and burden to bear, my aloneness, to choose or not to choose language. In many ways the work of writing this book is my effort to take seriously her trust, to make decisions about what to share and what not to share, to "give back," as she had once said of her motivation for our work in hopes that what is here, ultimately, might drive others into their own uncertainties, their own messy work, their own deep collaborations. At the same time, I see my project as an enactment of paradox and failure: in fact we simply can't ever be known and yet not encounter pain, complexity, and contradiction, ours or others'. This tension and deep contradiction is lifeblood in feminist rhetorical research and writing: we must engage complexity in representation in ways that inevitably reveal our losses, our damage, our gaps, so that we can forge new roads for understanding.

Dark Energy

This book is a disciplinary boundary-crosser that takes root in the discipline of rhetoric-composition, which, I'd argue, is already meant to exist on fault lines and in middle spaces. Still, I do struggle to contextualize this work as it draws on such multiple and separate disciplinary universes, though all ultimately in the service of feminist rhetorical studies. While I will return to the tensions of disciplinary categorization later in the book, it's worth noting here that this project is diversely informed through feminist methodology, medical rhetorics, rhetoric of science, theories of collaboration and care, rhetorics of embodiment and disability, feminist psychoanalytic theory, queer theory, theories of subjectivity and composing, and narrative medicine. Most important is this book's unique claims to feminist rhetorical research as an act of intimacy and, further, to intimacy as methodology.[4] What might research and writing look like, and how might knowledge take shape, in a practice (method) of intimacy as epistemology, as a way of writing through otherwise unspoken, even frightening, questions?

My use of the term "intimacy" is meant to be provocative, to invite us to think of blurred boundaries, of being even dangerously close to each other: collapsed walls between the personal, the academic, and the analytic. For example, what sorts of analytical arguments might be produced when I explore academic concepts—like research methodology, for example—in personal contexts? How might we rethink the use and process of interviewing, of working with transcripts, of how we read academic texts, when we let in uniquely personal experiences of memory, love, pain, and grief?[5] What happens when we refuse to operate in only one arena or mode at a time? It is in this context that this project travels the greatest distance, pushes most deeply on our relationship to what words can do, and challenges us to reimagine how and why we write and do research. Of course, this notion of "how" is varied and complex. I do not aim to draw conclusions or disciplinary boundary lines or to propose a theory or firm method. I seek only to make space. For this reason, my writing in this book will move across possibilities, mixing the personal and the academic, the analytical and the reflective. Always there will be emotionality, as this collaboration—the project itself—marks one of the great friendships of my life. I realize that here, too, I push: where do we draw the line between friendship and work, between love and research, between the private and the public? Why do we draw these lines at all? What might we gain and what might we lose?

I suppose the best answer to these questions is that I do not know. And this not-knowing is, for me, also at the core of this project. That this work holds at its center that which living people simply cannot fully know—dying—makes it a meditation on the limits of knowledge and on naming. It is meant to leave us all at least somewhat in the dark, to ask us to work within paradox. Inquiry into science and material embodiment has of course long acknowledged the limits of language. In a documentary about his life, the physicist Richard Feynman recounts his childhood curiosity about the backward movement of a ball in a wagon as it was pulled forward. "Why is that?" the young Feynman asks his father. "That," his father replies, "nobody knows." Feynman's father goes on to explain, "The general principle . . . is called 'inertia,' but nobody knows why it's true." Feynman categorizes his father's treatment here as evidence of "a deep understanding—the difference between knowing the name of something and knowing something." As a counterexample, he offers the memory task of learning the word for "bird" in multiple languages: "You'll only know about humans and what they call the bird. . . . You will know nothing whatsoever of the bird" (*Richard Feynman*).

In fact, to understand deeply may mean to touch the ceiling of what we can know at any one moment, to ultimately not see any further. Rhetoric is the vehicle by which we discover these limits and humbly own them. In her memoir, *A Body, Undone*, which explores with honest grief her experience of spinal cord injury and paralysis, Christina Crosby describes the act of writing in ways that capture its very inexplicability:

> Writing, no matter about what subject, has its way with the writer. . . .
> Writing offers, not a way out, but a way into the impossible dilemmas
> of not-knowing. Each sentence begun can wander off, sometimes ir-
> retrievably into confusion and mistake, sometimes to greater clarity.
> . . . Writing works on memory, compressing and doubtless distorting
> the past, and offers bodies for the inspection of reader and writer
> alike. (200)

At root here is a twofold reality: the limits of knowledge and the limits of identity and subjectivity. Reader and writer—both inspecting and under inspection—are never of course the "same" in standpoint, perspective, or experience. In "Aching for a Self," the under-studied rhetorician Jim Corder strips bare this tension with his question, "How do you compose yourself for another? . . . Perhaps there is no composing yourself for another, no matter what you do: you're always left behind by your own text" (267). In a sense—and here I believe is Crosby's point—the more we work to write ourselves into both understanding and being understood, the more inevitably we are to contend with our losses, with what we can't do or communicate, with the limits of shared experience, the intersection of language and body.

Surely explorations of the rhetorics of historiography, method, and embodiment have already contributed substantively to these enduring tensions.[6] But my work in this book is to illustrate my own movement as a researcher, writer, and person into deeper, unfolding uncertainty and tension and then to insist on the value of staying there, as a way of affirming such spaces as foundational and fertile for feminist research, rhetoric, and writing. Risks and leaps of faith have been among the few "certainties" of my experience in this project. The sciences, rooted in a devotion to certainty, illustrate the stakes of such risk poignantly. In his 2012 article "New Secrets of the Universe," Brian Greene describes scientists' widening conception of space and our positioning in it, upending notions of our universe as solitary: "Our Universe [might be] a single expanding bubble inhabiting a grand cosmic bubble bath of universes—a multiverse" (23). Contending with the likelihood that such multiple universes, if they exist, are beyond our powers of observation, Greene explains that astronomers have hypothesized that these universes are pushing away from each other with something they call "dark energy." In an attempt to understand "how much dark energy would have to permeate every nook and cranny of space" to explain this distancing, astronomers "found a number that no one has been able to explain. Not even close" (23).

What has emerged, Green explains, is a vast disparity:

> Expressed in relevant units, the dark energy density is extraordinary small. . . . At the same time, attempts by researchers to calculate the amount of dark energy from the laws of physics have yielded results that are typically a hundred orders of magnitude larger, perhaps the greatest mismatch between observation and theory in the history of science. (23)

Thus at the very center of efforts to understand is a mathematical disconnect, a gap; there are suddenly no reliable tools for understanding or certainty. My collaboration with Sue began with a similarly impossible chasm: her desire to be known and yet not to hurt anyone (perhaps even herself). Now I too face an impasse: to render her, to honor her wish to be known, but only with an imperfect capacity and amid the very pain she sought to spare those she loved.

Such "mismatch," the presence of a permanent impasse, is fertile soil for this book, which explores how and why we move forward when things simply do not make easy or predictable sense or when our previously reliable processes fail us. Jay Dolmage's work in disability rhetorics offers us hopeful space for "a critical modality . . . that recognizes cultures and individuals, as well as any interpretive act itself, as essentially disabled, prosthetic" (287). What Greene describes as a mismatch between observation and theory invites an inventive tension, a conceptual leap of sorts beyond the limits or even comfort of "knowing." He questions, "What role could other universes possibly play in science, a discipline devoted to explaining what we do see?" (23). I might respond by pointing to Dolmage's challenge to interpretation, which at root asks us to suspend our belief in what we observe and to commit instead to the possibility that there is simply more or at least always "other" beyond our own abilities to understand or to make sense. This interpretative approach is not only about physical disability or the failure of the body, as in terminal illness, but, I would argue, also a way of thinking about methodology and disciplinarity. I am reminded here of Feynman's critique of naming—bird versus bird—and the observation of the phenomenon or principle of inertia. What do we do with such gaps? Where do we go from here?

Greene admits that the mathematical mismatch around dark energy "has led to some soul searching" for scientists (23). I want to stay here— *soul searching*—as a way into this book. As researchers and writers, we are shuttled into such a practice only when we admit that our standard methods have failed us. I believe that there is a great energy, what I would call in the case of this book a unique kind of knowledge making, that is possible if we allow ourselves to remain at least partially in the dark. And by "dark" in this case I mean of course that we accept a mismatch between how we attempt to understand (method) and what we are ultimately able to fully learn, that we pursue the paradox of the desire to know or be known and the corresponding risk of hurt. This book thus tours my own efforts and failures, and it works out of a kind of permanent darkness: that which we cannot fully comprehend and that from which we cannot fully heal. I thus argue for broken methods and contradiction, for creativity and too much feeling, for blurred genres and for doing the work that scares us. My goal is to refuse to cover up, to deny the reader—and myself—protection from my own inadequacies as journey partner, word to word and hour to hour into the end of a life. I welcome readers to this book in the spirit of paradox: one of human desire, of research, and of writing. My hope is not for the emergence of any new, singular method for doing our work but rather to model and encourage the practice of becoming ourselves through our work, that is, allowing the process of doing the work—however that must happen—to teach us to become *new* writers, researchers, friends. In essence, I call for work that makes us human, over and over again.

Structure of the Book

The remaining chapters of the book consider theory and approach to feminist research and writing using narrative moments from our collaboration in the last two years of Sue's illness as critical junctures for rethinking, reinvestigating, and ideally reinventing the role of researcher/writer/collaborator as well as the texts we might produce. I often revisit a story or moment multiple times throughout the book, looping back again in a recursive process central to writing-as-thinking and connection. Accordingly, in the chapters themselves I move non-linearly through Sue's experiences—and often through my own reflective writings in response to sharing many of those experiences by her side—while stopping to consider theoretical shifts and foundations worthy of either continued building or reconsideration. I do this using the concept of "surrender" as a conceptual lever, which I establish and explore most fully in the "Stage III" chapter. "Surrender," a notion Sue and I discussed often as her illness worsened, functions in this book as a way of continually insisting on a kind of letting go, a release, not only of what we already know how to do (practice) and what we think we know (epistemology) but also of our subjectivit(ies) as writers and researchers. For my own part, at times I let go of the narrative, and at other times I release myself, as a writer, from what I might consider the more traditionally "academic." Often I bounce back and forth in ways I find inadequate. As I have reworked and reread this manuscript, my movements from academic analysis to intimate narrative and then back again often feel like transgressions, even as I weave them together. I have chosen to let these be so that others can feel and understand from their diverse standpoints.

My risk here is my own surrendering in text as an extension or representation of the lived experience I shared with my friend through her illness. However banal the claim that, as rhetors, writers, and re-searchers, we often seek control, my sense is that interrogation and destabilization of this longing for control is essential, continuous work. Accordingly, in the first formal chapter in the book, "Stage IV. Making Space: Methodology and the Search for Ourselves," I begin with a meditation on Jim Corder's decades-old search for a stable, writerly subject and move into a discussion of the unique challenges this project poses to such hopes for control. I consider the largely cisgendered male, heteronormative tradition of autoethnography and adopt instead Jacqueline Rhodes and Jonathan Alexander's insistence on a queer subject position that embraces the "unknowable" (Rhodes, "Rhizomes"). In "Stage III. Rooting Surrender: Rhythm, Dissonance, and Letting Go in the Research Process," I draw on psychoanalytic feminist theorist Jessica Benjamin's use of the term "surrender" and its connection, for Benjamin, to the concept of intersubjectivity as a way of exploring or allowing for transformative work between research collaborators in ways that, I argue, are practically representative of Rhodes and Alexander's theoretical frame. In "Stage II. Building and Breaking: Methodological Contradictions and Unanswerable Questions," I press critically on Peter Smagorinsky's claim that "studies work best when an author poses a limited set of answerable questions and then designs the paper around them" ("Method Section" 405). I argue that the interpretative challenges posed by research and writing amid illness and intimacy demand a methodological break from Smagorinsky's framework that roots analysis in a humanities-focused lens even while culling primary source materials through qualitative research practices (like interviewing and transcription). I offer as a critical alternative Lisa Mazzei's work in education research in which she traces a moment of "troubling resistance" posed by traditional methods of transcription and coding in her own work as a social scientist ("Silent Listenings" 29). I try to demonstrate the ways in which a failure to honor and also pursue this "troubling resistance" through methodological surrender limits our work and what we might learn by fuller investigation of language, and most importantly of our own researcher-writer selves, on the edges of illness and intimacy.

After closing the "Stage II" chapter with an application for a reflexive interview practice, I shift my focus in "Stage I. Radical Care: Rhetorical Bodies in Contact" to the role of rhetorical touch and physical care in constructing a methodology for, as Patti Lather has written, "getting lost" (203). This notion of "getting lost" is in many ways an exercise in destabilizing bodies (and "bodies" can include researcher-participant bodies but also bodies of data and text) and coming to know these bodies as capable of illness, destruction, loss, and not-knowing. Among others, I consider Shannon Walters's research on rhetorics of touch and Jay Dolmage's emphasis on exnomination in the construction of disability, as well as Max Van Manen's work in the phenomenology of illness, in order to examine the rhetorical transaction uniquely possible between bodies, healthy and ill, in the dying process. I frame three concepts relevant to an embodied researcher-participant *dynamis* that make possible ethical approaches to work that overwhelms us physically, emotionally, and intellectually.

The last chapter of the book takes steps toward a fuller examination of both the conceptual and the practical, ultimately inviting (and enacting) methods for our work that I hope most fully challenge our boundaries. I begin this final chapter, "In Situ. Love as Frame," with a return to Jim Corder's work through a memorial essay written by his former student Elizabeth Ervin following his death. For Corder and for Ervin, love has a necessary place in rhetorical work as the space in which we "speak and write . . . arguments . . . that will make us plain to all others, thoughtful histories and narratives that reveal us as we're reaching for the others" (Corder, "Argument" 31). In my rendering, this "plainness" reveals love—and the lover—as broken and incomplete but also, as such, evolving, and thus the researcher-who-loves as human, confused, fraught, and generative. Research and writing that emerge from such a place employ tools that sometimes fail due to our own limitations, a testament to both our reaching—*longing*, as Rhodes might call it—and the impossibility of our arrival at total understanding or full representation of any other. In the second half of this chapter I pull forward many of the concepts explored throughout the book, including the role of time, of a shifting researcher-participant *dynamis*, and of "bad data," or that which scares or overwhelms us, and pose a series of applicable questions for those interested in doing similar kinds of work. I resist throughout the book, but especially in the last chapter, the setting up of reductive debates or hierarchies. I am not arguing here for "better" or more superior methods, nor am I attempting to make sweeping claims about what research is or should be. I am instead pressing the importance of doing fine-grained work and affirming the unique value of work that fails to protect us from pain or loss. My hope is that my sharing this project might encourage others to embrace similar kinds of research collaborations when they arise rather than to dismiss these exigencies as too emotional, too personal, or just not "real" research. Love, as a practice and a concept, makes room for our diversions and eccentricities. It accepts our assumptions and celebrates our shortcomings as inventive, and, with care, love resists our cleaner, more predictable lines. Thus this last chapter brings the project full circle, reaffirming both a synthesis of methods and, most importantly, a reversal of roles—researcher and researched, writer and written about—and emphasizing the relevancy of methodological diversity, the necessity of the personal, and the analytical richness of unpredictability and risk in being who we are in our work at any given moment, particularly in extraordinary circumstances that test our many limits. This book enacts a textured, small-scale study, employing qualitative-style methods with the sort of analytical seeking that desires contact with our borders, and the creation of new kinds of writing, methods, and roles inscribed by these very boundary lines.

BLOODWORK
(A LETTER TO CANCER)

Hello Cancer . . .

Why are you here? What are you trying to teach me, or do you really care? You frighten the hell out of me and I don't want to be afraid. I have kids that need me . . . why are you here?

Why have you decided to "wake up" and why are you growing in my body? What is your purpose? What is your goal? How come my body doesn't treat you like the invader you appear to be?

I find it hard to believe with all the technology out there that they haven't found a way to stop you from taking the lives of so many people. Why do you do that? Is that your goal? Are you misunderstood or are you that obnoxious bully?

I don't want to fear you. I want to understand you. I am open to any and all lessons that you are here to teach me, if that is your purpose . . . but I'm not so sure about that. I know there will be lessons learned regardless, but I'm not so sure that is what you are here to do. So why are you here?

Thank you for leaving my organs alone, and thank you for NOT *eating away at my bone. Please do not take away my ability to be active and to run. I don't really require much, but that is something that makes me feel so alive.*

What does this all mean anyway? The crazy thing is that I feel healthier than I've ever felt and I feel physically stronger than I've ever been as well . . . it's such a crazy irony. The scans tell me I have cancer and apparently it's in more spots than originally mentioned. It's hard to believe at times. . . . Now I'm told that I have to change medications because what I was taking is no longer working. It's the craziest mind game of all time. By the way, how do you figure out a work-around? Obviously there is some intelligence going on here. How long does it take before you figure it out? Do you get excited when you conquer the drugs, or is it more like when water just keeps wearing away the sides of a river until it finally change its course?

I hate the thought of having my life cut short by something I have no control over and that I don't understand. I'm willing to do whatever I need to. . . . I'm willing to accept all the challenges that come with your existence. . . . My biggest worry, however, is that the effort put forth to overcome these challenges will not really matter in the end; that they are not life lessons . . . that to me would be the cruelest joke of all of this . . . that the hoops that you make people go through to live is mere entertainment for you and that when all is said and done, you get the last laugh, "watch what I can get this idiot to do now . . . watch how desperate they become . . . wait until the pleading starts . . . that's my favorite . . . hahaha." If that is true, then you deserve a huge FUCK YOU. . . .

I don't want to die . . . apparently you don't want to either . . . so can we come to a place where we can live in harmony? Why do we have to fight to the death? Why does it have to be an "either or" situation?

So, I am going to do everything I can to live and to live well. If that means that we cannot coexist, then so be it. I don't remember inviting you in, and I'm not happy about you hanging around, but if you feel the need to stay, then I ask you to please respect my body, and when you do decide to go, please do not take me with you . . .

Susan Lundy Maute
September 2013

STAGE IV

MAKING SPACE

METHODOLOGY AND THE SEARCH FOR OURSELVES

In an effort to describe his grandmother's practice of quilt making, the rhetorician Jim Corder tells us first that she was poor and illiterate with eyes "desperately weak and crossed" ("I in Mine" 259). Her quilts were made "without the aid of authors who want to be sure that the world gets corrected . . . to be sure we define the quiltmaker's art in their way" and with only accumulated scraps since she had no money to buy materials (259). Still, Corder tells of her intricate process, one that produced quilts "beautifully rendered" where "without design, she made design" (260). Corder's story is important for two reasons relevant to this book: it is a meditation on method and methodology, and it is something of a flailing expression of the human desire to witness, to record, and to recognize and be recognized, however or whatever the depiction. Of the latter, Corder confesses his anxiety: "If I don't remember her, and try to get her down right, she will vanish" (260). Such anxiety of memory has its roots of course in the inevitable, slippery quality of memory itself: the experience of being the only one—the last one, maybe—to remember something or someone "right" combines with the futility of that very subject position. Even if memory won't quite die with us—we've told our stories—we can't control the reception, the audience, or our widening, temporal distance from the person or the event we most want to hold close.[1] Corder asks, "Who else will tell what you remember and try to make it real but you?" (260). There's an honest, human desperation to what he describes as "the desire to hold some things from oblivion" (260).

Honest human desire is not without its exploits, and certainly what we desire—to be known, to have our beloveds remembered through

19

us—can overwhelm our view, obscure our ability to see beyond our own needs and experiences. Sensitive to such possibility by the close of his story, Corder notes self-consciously, "I understand that this may be a selfish, self-serving conception, a way of calling attention to oneself. I understand that I may be trapped in the aspirations of what some call radical individualism" (260). It is not just "Grandma Corder" he strives to record, to "get down right," but also himself—at least, some written, textual version of himself, what he values and remembers, in this case. Still though, in admitting this personal desire Corder circles back once again to its futility: "I know that in trying to hold things, I too will vanish. I had hoped to be real, but I am only a vacancy in the air" (260). In one fell swoop, he ties together a set of desires and also methodological problems relevant, I will argue, to how we write and do research: the push to capture, to tell the story, to be the witness and to *have been* witnessed collide inevitably with our need for audiences and contexts. In fact, part and parcel with the need to tell and show is the necessity of letting go, releasing our story into the world so that it might be known. As soon as Corder crafts "Grandma Corder," renders her in text, she is cast out to others—readers, audiences—capable of recognizing her and also of forgetting her, debating Corder's rendition, or perhaps even writing their own, more "accurate" picture. As we seek recognition—"the desire to hold some things from oblivion"—we also suffer a kind of loss. We can't keep the story, or our research, all for ourselves if we want it known, valued, seen, heard.

This is a well-worn meditation on memory, subjectivity, and representation, though certainly I think it continues to be relevant to all of us who do such writing work and who want to do it with reflexivity. Still, Corder—whose writing from the 1960s into the 1990s (later anthologized) remains under-studied in rhetoric-composition—strikes a particular nerve, one that offers what I will argue is a key entry point into conversations about our relationship to method and methodology as writers and researchers.[2] While he clings to the personal, to his right to capture things, he also represents and exalts a method, *Grandma Corder's process* of making. As he does this, he simultaneously diminishes the "authors," the "experts" we might call them, anticipating that they will devalue this process, since their work is to "correct." Grandma Corder doesn't need them; she has her own method, and his job, as her ethnographer, is to capture it, to create a record that flies in the face of what has been written and otherwise labeled "art." He overturns established authorities as he claims, "Without design, she made design." We might argue here that Corder does much the same as those "authors" he criticizes: all try to "get [it] down right." This might be why, at least in part, he is aware of the futility of his efforts: "I know that in trying to hold things, I too will vanish." Corder, all at once, has created and also overturned method; with this move, he's guaranteed the same fate for his own design, his own method.

As scholars, many of us have made such efforts to capture, defend, or proscribe methods for our work in hopes that others will remember, look and listen, follow suit. Indeed, in rhetoric-composition we share conjoined fields (hence the hyphen) whose histories are both short and long, with practical and conceptual tentacles reaching from the humanities to the social sciences, with methods qualitative and quantitative, historical, analytical. My aim in this book is to stake out some space for a story about research and writing that might dislocate us in useful ways from what we already know, from what we see more easily as our methodological roads and possibilities, our myriad ways of doing our work. More specifically, my goal is to pursue the very slipperiness Corder laments in the roles we construct for ourselves as researchers and writers, in our expectations for the work we produce, and in our sense of what we might learn from what we do as scholars. Where does research live when these expectations, these boundary lines, are not just redrawn but lost? Under what circumstances might we find ourselves, amid our own Corder-like attempts to capture and hold tight, truly relocated, flung into foreign territory as scholars but also as people? At root, I believe such dislocation is possible, necessary, in some of the richest, most challenging kinds of research work and that, especially for those of us whose work is bound up with words and their capacity to render human suffering, we must carve out some space, make methodological room in which we can allow the unfamiliar to stay that way, to give permission of sorts for our own delivery into oblivion. This is as much about method as it is about "who" we can become as writing, researching subjects. It is in peering over these most jagged, most uncertain edges that, I will argue, we might learn more fully about language, about our connection to each other and to ourselves in words.

There are more theoretical and practical connections available here than I can reasonably or responsibly make; I am aware that I cannot be comprehensive. I thus want to begin with Susan Wells's *Our Bodies, Ourselves and the Work of Writing*, as it paves a topical inroad into the story at the core of this book, which is a story about illness, loss, and friendship. Wells's project in *Our Bodies* is analysis of the numerous iterations and processes around the well-known women's movement health resource book *Our Bodies, Ourselves*, written collaboratively by the Boston Women's Health Collective. In the "Postscript" to the book, she reflects on the experience of having her own manuscript draft "marked up" by members of "the collective":

> Eventually, I realized that the collective's last gift to me was this mark up of my own draft, peremptory and a little obsessive, delivered over in faith that the text that two or three writers hashed out would be better than what any one writer could do. . . . I had been inducted into the collective's writing process. (211)

Perhaps most poignantly, Wells goes on to explain the challenges that came with this "induction":

> I was used to struggling to represent the nuances of my own under-standing, to taking full responsibility for my text and all that it said. For me, the coherence of the book from page to page and from chapter to chapter was an expression of my personal integrity. (212)

Given its capacity for collective action and its necessary destabilizing of the control of any single author—perhaps in some ways this is a de-stabilizing of coherence itself—"collective writing," as Wells delivers it to us, allows us to understand that "some of the most significant work we can do as rhetoricians concerns speakers and writers who are ready, willing, and able to talk back" (212). These conversations are "both unruly and generative," and the "scholarship in rhetoric" that ensues is "in a way, a huge babble of conversation among researchers and those they study" (212).

In the "unruly and generative," Wells widens our frame, creating possibility for our work that allows in the messiness of subjectivity, of our entwined, potentially complicated relationships to our own roles and to each other, researcher and researched, writer and written-about. My focus in this book is a collaborative ethnography that turned me—as researcher/writer—essentially inside out and at times incoherent, making my own processes for coming to understand, for finding my way in words, foreign and essentially requiring of me new ways of coming to the work of rhetorical analysis and writing. In the summer of 2012, I began an ethnography project with Susan Lundy Maute, a woman living at the time with terminal breast cancer. Sue and I were friends, teammates in fact, playing in a women's field hockey league most months of the year. She was a talented athlete and had played elite-level lacrosse and field hockey in her college days. She was the mother of four children. Sue had first been diagnosed with breast cancer at the young age of thirty-five, six months following the birth of her fourth child. Through surgeries, radiation, and chemo, she had lived with her disease for over a decade; she lived at stage IV, "terminal," for five tremendous years, during which she played competitive field hockey with fit, healthy twenty-somethings, bounding from chemo to the field. She stunned me, just absolutely stunned me. And we found ourselves often in step: on monthly hikes with a group of friends, we'd keep pace, lost in talk; on the sidelines after our hockey games, we'd stand together, always in conversation. We had an easy, rolling dialogue, and we shared a language that athletes know, thickly tuned to the body and the joys of pushing it, which seemed to make talking about her illness a natural extension of our chatter.[3]

This book will trace key moments in our collaborative work, which began formally in the last two years of Sue's life when I invited her to visit a class I was teaching, Rhetoric of Sport, to discuss her unique relationship to sport and the body. The course syllabus posed a series of questions linking language and physical accomplishment, such as, "How are athletic 'heroes' constructed in words? In what ways do athletes rely on language to explain or even understand their own bodily performances?" (Restaino, "Syllabus"). Class discussion moved quickly from celebrity athletes to nontraditional ones: octogenarian track stars and amputees, the image of gold-medal hopeful Derek Redmond completing the 400m at the Barcelona Olympics despite a torn hamstring, aided by his father to the finish line.[4] Sue embodied a similar spirit and, after writing a short piece my students read in advance about her illness and her history as an athlete, joined us for a class discussion. During that class visit, we found ourselves easily engaging relevant concepts on the course syllabus with Sue's writing and experiences, and students were transfixed by her appearance as "well" and her physical drive despite her terminal status. Sue and I were quickly shuttled into a new kind of relationship. Ultimately we would travel together to her very last hours—in talk, in writing, physically present for and with each other in some of the hardest moments and tied to an ethnography project the goals of which continued to shift and expand.

In our beginnings, at a moment when Sue was terminal but stable, both of us aware of the magic of that class visit and also of our own deepening dialogue, we agreed to keep talking, to pursue more formally a series of interviews and writings around her experience. But I worried:

What exactly were we doing, anyway, and why? Why follow the seeds of our natural connection, the richness of her visit to my class, in a series of interviews and writings between friends? I worried that Sue was just being generous with me, indulging my interest in language and its relationship to the body, my admiration of her mental toughness and of her way of finding the words that allowed her to think through her experience and push forward. But why, amid a struggle for her own survival, should she indulge me? Surely she had bigger interests to attend to: her children, her treatment, her evolving disease. *She is a giving sort*, I told myself, as I wrote up questions for us each to answer about the purpose and goals of our work. *What if she is just doing me a favor and what if, in a way I didn't intend, I am being coercive?* At the very same moment a contradictory question also haunted me: *What if she wants to keep talking and writing? What if this could help her in some way and yet I withhold it because of my own self-doubt?*

I entered this work aware of both the efforts and valid anxieties of feminist scholars around mutuality and the challenges of authority in the research process. In her 2005 essay "Friendship, Friendliness, and Feminist Fieldwork," Gesa Kirsch reminds us that participants often "want to 'help' the researcher" and that interviews are "likely to be asymmetrical interactions, with one party—the party generally with the most institutional power—asking the questions and the other answering" (2165). Kirsch assumes, rightly, that most researcher-participant collaborations are not built first on friendship and that oftentimes participants begin to perceive or feel a kind of friendliness toward the researcher. It makes human sense: "Appreciating the undivided attention, sincere interest, and warmth shown by skillful interviewers . . . participants can easily reveal intimate details about their lives that they may later regret having shared" (2164). Quoting Pamela Cotterill, Kirsch offers this harsh reminder: "Close friends do not usually arrive with a tape-recorder, listen carefully and sympathetically to what you have to say and then disappear" (2166).

In order to pave a way forward, I must first slice the Cotterill quotation into at least two parts: I did sometimes arrive with a tape recorder, though not always; but I did not ever disappear. In fact, I stayed all the way until Sue's final hours, on my knees beside her bed, her face in my hands, my thumb pressed to her forehead. Being present was something she had asked of me, and by then I would not have had it any other way. I suppose however that a part of me has in fact vanished, and perhaps much in the way Corder worries about: we were two, a pair, struggling together to make linguistic sense, to find the words for the experience of her increasingly threatening and complex illness and, finally, for her death. Our work was that of a shared desire to understand, to put words to experience, but it also was a work of friendship and love. There is no "getting it right" on my own now, despite hours of recorded and transcribed conversations, and there is no return to the private space of our collaboration, our talk and writing about her experience of illness, of living and dying with breast cancer.

Amid my admission here of an inevitable failure of sorts, I want to make the concurrent argument that such failure, such aloneness, such struggle through loss in words is, indeed, worthy research, worthy of our attention if we want to understand how language functions to usher us through some of the most necessary, most profound experiences of our lives. This, too, is rhetorical work. It is not—of course—the "only" or somehow reductively the "best" kind of study; that is not my argument. But it has a rightful place in our repertoire of work in feminist rhetorical studies. Toward the end of her essay, Kirsch posits that "we need to develop more realistic—and perhaps more limited—expectations about relationships with participants" (2168). I join her call here for more realistic expectations, though from the other side of the room: I ask here that, as researchers and writers, we find greater analytical space for love, for friendship, for care, for being changed and lost and rewritten ourselves in the research process. I call not for irresponsibility and recklessness with participants—in fact I think Kirsch's warnings are wise and ought to be largely obeyed—but for critical attunement, attention, and openness so that we might recognize those unique collaborations that have the capacity for overpowering and destabilizing *us*, for teaching us new rhetorical limits. Friendship and love are, too, fertile ground for the study of rhetoric.[5]

The entwined, complex roots of our project found their seeds in a few questions I wrote for Sue and me to each answer separately, in writing, in an effort to articulate goals for our work. The plan was that we would each write from our own perspective and then share with the other. I began this document with the course description from my original syllabus as a point of reflection, an anchor into the class visit that started our more formal conversation. In response to my first question, which asked each of us to explain our "initial understanding of the purpose of our conversations," Sue wrote, "I came with a completely open mind and decided to let your questions guide the dialog" (Maute, "Project Purpose Response"). This response positioned me clearly in a researcher role, a role with which I was already struggling. In my own response to the same prompt, I wrote,

> I've found myself asking questions for which I knew perhaps neither Sue nor I had any simple answers (or perhaps any answers at all), and so it's fair to say that in some ways we've moved away from focused research and more towards a kind of investigative, conversational journey. (Restaino, "Project Purpose Response")

While I had initially positioned myself as the qualitative researcher I vaguely knew how to be (more on that later), I soon found myself struggling within the strictures of that role. I wrote interview questions, but we went off the script quickly. In part this was because though I tried to anticipate some possibilities for Sue's responses to the questions I posed—about the relationship between language and the body, between illness and athleticism—she routinely upended me, took me to places conceptually I could not go on my own by virtue of the space between our experiences.

There was, even early on, a compelling draw or pull to this foreign territory for me. But the space between us was never a question, so demarcated as it was by our occupation of uniquely different female bodies. Despite our shared racial identities as white women—Sue, fair and freckled with Irish heritage, and me, olive-skinned given my southern Italian roots—we were physically separated by health and illness, by surgical intervention, and by our respective orientations to time and the expectations for its unfolding.[6] Early in our work I worried quite a lot about the risks and the challenges to mutuality. I followed the first question about the purpose of our conversations with a prompt about personal meaning in the project. I felt compelled to ask, "Can you describe the value, if any, of our conversations to *you*? What purpose or point might they serve for you?" (Restaino, "Project Purpose Response"). I wanted to make space in which Sue could voice some negative comments, admit her own disconnection, or where I could at least listen for her hesitancy, her possible hedging, maybe a worrisome politeness. I thus added a caveat, "(It's okay if the answer is 'none' beyond 'helping Jess with a project')." Sue's response instead affirmed her own stake in our work together:

> Having come with no expectation, I have to say I was blown away at how much I got out of our conversations. It's very hard to see what I look like from outside of this body and mind without having some kind of external feedback. From my perspective, I'm just doing what I

need to do with what I've been handed, nothing more. (Maute, "Project
Purpose Response")

In an email in advance of this writing, Sue offered, "I enjoy sharing
all of this, it helps confirm for me that there is more to all of this than
me being just another victim of the big 'C'" (Maute, "Re: Direction").
These two texts were the first to indicate that our work together had
some potential value for Sue beyond the scope of my original invitation
to talk with students about her experience of living with breast cancer
as an athlete.

But perhaps equally striking is my writing in response to this same
prompt. I was, at the time, so concerned with Sue's experience that I
overlooked in some ways my own. In fact, the private space of our dialogue was one in which I found tremendous security, a surprising sense
of calm and gratitude despite the gravity of the situation. For my part,
I wrote the following explanation, which I'll quote at length:

> I think our conversations have taken me to a level of thought that
> many living without chronic or life-threatening conditions often avoid
> or ignore. Our discussions have forced me to think about the brevity
> of the lifespan (even when it's lived out to its lengthier possibilities),
> the potential vulnerability of the body, the medical field . . . and many
> other weighty subjects. These topics have pushed me, and they are on
> my mind long after any of our conversations end. While the feelings
> they stir up are sometimes painful ones, I also don't regret any of it.
> I feel like, in "going there," even when I could otherwise avoid or
> ignore it (even as this tendency in itself is a kind of self-deceit since
> we all contend with mortality), I have gained some kind of intellectual
> clarity or stability or control that I might not otherwise have. I feel
> less afraid, less intimidated by these big issues. (Restaino, "Project
> Purpose Response")

My multiple roles—researcher, writer, friend—were often in motion,
moving back and forth between us, and my "intellectual clarity or stability or control" was rooted in a situation, by its very existence, that
precisely resisted control. This dynamic raises questions not only about
methodology and collaboration but also about disability, bodies, and
access. In this book I will attempt to consider these questions in light
of the particulars of our relationship, informed by a variety of scholarly
voices. For now, I ask that we make room, honor, and allow the "unruly and generative" that Wells's work grants us. My goal is to build

on and deepen conversations about feminist method and methodology by offering up a boundary-pushing model. Our work happened in the private spaces of illness, friendship, and death and stretched to certain depths I had never visited nor imagined before in my writing or lived experience. Such work calls not only for a unique brand of mutuality but for an investigation of the shifting researcher role occasioned by inquiry into the unknown.

Excavating the Researcher: Subjectivity, Expressivism, and the Personal

The investigation I'm calling for here requires a return of sorts to a consideration of our subjectivity, as researchers but also as writers, in ways that I'd argue we've moved quite far from in rhetoric-composition. Such subjectivity includes (but also critically revisits) not only feminist discussions of care, a topic I'll examine at some length in a later chapter, but also a return to our field's valuing of the personal, a tradition in composition studies, in particular, that I believe has largely failed to find its way beyond primary discussions of teaching alone.[7] At the 2015 Conference on College Composition and Communication, I attended a panel that included Lad Tobin and Thomas Newkirk, both longtime proponents of teaching personal narrative, the inclusion of which, for both, affirms the value and place of students' stories as inherent in their learning to make and advance academic arguments. Attention to personal writing in the field has surely waned overall, particularly as our interests have become more diverse and the options for our study have multiplied. This shift in focus isn't new, of course, and Tobin's talk addressed the shift decisively, noting the pervasive, negative attitude that "personal narrative was fine in its time" before the move to "'real' academic work, to rigor" (Tobin, "Telling the Tales"). Corder, of course, was uniquely interested in the personal and struggled somewhat mightily with the rise of scholarship on collaborative writing in the field in the mid-1980s. His meditation on Grandma Corder speaks to his belief in writing from a largely singular perspective, in the validity of his own experience; such belief shapes his writings on pedagogy as well.[8]

In his 2014 *Minds Made for Stories*, Newkirk reaffirms our natural affinity for narrative, and its value as a teaching tool for both writers and readers, stretching even to the challenges of understanding the sciences. He explains, "Photosynthesis is a story; climate change is a story; cancer is a story, with antecedents and consequences" (11). Advancing toward technique and a consideration of the writer's subjectivity,

Newkirk quotes Wayne Booth on the writer's unique task of constructing readers—"'the author makes his readers'"—and, "'if he makes them
well—that is he makes them see what they have never seen before, moves
them into a new order of perception and experience altogether—he
finds his reward in the peers he has created'" (15). Newkirk goes on to
lament our field's tendency to present "form or a visual structure" rather
than "a series of moves" in how we understand or teach narrative writing. Pulling readers forward, beckoning that we follow his own moves,
Newkirk writes at once playfully and seriously:

> Because I am asking you (are you still there?) to keep with me for the
> next 150 pages, this is a very real issue. Like Walt Whitman I want
> you to believe that "I am with you and know how it is." (18)

Immediately in Newkirk's even playful phrasing we can hear two
qualities clearly reminiscent of Corder's earlier writing on his grandmother: a desire for personal authority and recognition and an anxiety
about loss. Newkirk worries he'll lose his readers ("are you still there?"),
but perhaps most poignantly his desire, mixed possibly with anxiety,
is one laden with subjectivity and ethos: "I want you to believe that 'I
am with you and know how it is.'" Whitman's lines from "Crossing
Brooklyn Ferry," which also serve as an opening epigraph for Newkirk's
chapter, assign a kind of heightened authority to this desire, making it
not only a human one but one that has sustained over time, validated by
a literary giant. We all want to connect; we all want to be understood;
we all want to be awarded a kind of knowledge or authority ("I . . . know
how it is") that assigns us credibility with readers (or the masses or our
friends and so on). However, in this moment, on this page, the desire
belongs to Newkirk, the writer, and the connection—"I want you to
believe"—is about the need for recognition, for affirmation of the very
human need for authority, for subjectivity.[9] In Corder, this anxious
desire surfaces in his reflections on the importance and need for his
story about his grandmother: "If I don't remember her, and try to get
her down right, she will vanish." There is, after all, no one to write, or
at least claim, such subjectivity: "Who else will tell what you remember
and try to make it real but you?" Newkirk not only affirms this impulse;
he reveals its very dependency on external validation, on audience, on
witness. The fact of narrative form falls here into the shadow of a search
for self, expression, and recognition.

But this search is one rooted in stability, which expects stability in
the writer, researcher, storyteller, and self. Still, Newkirk offers some

flexibility or room for error in our renderings of narrative reality, noting a kind of inevitable gap in reporting. He writes,

> It's ok to come close, to get most if it (even the word *approximation*—being proximate, close to—shows how seductive the metaphor of space is!). . . . Perfection is a bitch and not really the right goal anyway. (*Minds* 144)

While nearness, our ability to recreate what was as closely as possible (at least, as it exists in the subjective, writerly mind), may be "seductive," as Newkirk claims, what in fact *is* the "right goal" of narrative and the personal? Newkirk offers a reasonable and broad stroke: "We are caught in time, caught in history. Or rather, history is the form we give to time. . . . We rely on stories not merely for entertainment, but for explanation, meaning, self-understanding" (145). While Newkirk sees narrativity in all we do, in fact many of us may not identify our work as such, or at least not primarily, fundamentally so. While I would argue that in both Newkirk and Corder we find an anxious linking of the personal to time itself—time moves, of course, and so the slippage of our narrative foothold is guaranteed—what I think undergirds this anxiety is far more important. And that is a preoccupation with an imperfect self, a resistance, really, to a broken, overwhelmed, multiple writerly subjectivity.

Hitched to narrative, we find a search or longing for "self-understanding" amid a tense struggle with time: either to untie ourselves from its grasp (Corder) or in fact to harness it (Newkirk). To that end, I want to push here on Newkirk's "metaphor of space" via Corder's meditation on the same subject. Newkirk claims narrative operates as a "form" we assign to time, yet Corder approaches from a more defensive position. For Corder, time is endlessly out of our control. He explains, "Since we don't have time, we must rescue time by putting it into our discourses and holding it there" ("Argument as Emergence" 31). "Invention" is our effort, for Corder, "to speak and write not argumentative displays and presentations, but arguments . . . that will make us plain to all others, thoughtful histories and narratives that reveal as we're reaching for the others" (31). Such moves to "unbind time," to undo or "save" time, however fleetingly, from its own march are the moves of a fantastical "rescuer" subject, a savior in words. Newkirk's call for narrative shares Corder's devotion to this deeper, raw desire. Newkirk writes, "We seek the companionship of a narrator who maintains our

30

attention, and perhaps affection. We are not made for objectivity and pure abstraction—for timelessness" (*Minds* 146). While Corder hopes to unbind time from its incessant pace, keeping it somehow still in the space between us, Newkirk creates time, sets its pace, in the controlled space of narrative and the companionship with readers it demands. Both scramble in words, in the rendering of text, against a unique temporal powerlessness.

This swirling of narrative with our search for self-revelation—for being seen by others, for secure connection, and as a kind of salve to the "problem" of time—demands that we stretch in two seemingly contradictory directions if we accept any of what Corder and Newkirk posit: we need nearness and also *room*. By "room" I mean not only for others to be present, disruptive even, in our work as scholars but also for a kind of messiness and nonlinearity that far exceeds Newkirk's permission that we merely "come close." Well beyond accepting the impossibility of perfection in our personal renderings of experience (whether contained by temporal structure or not), I'd argue studies in rhetoric-composition have as of yet been shy of making full analytical, methodological use of the personal—by which I mean a willingness to consider the researcher-writer as undone, lost, out of control—because we have still too tightly aligned ourselves with comfortable orientations to both time and narrative, together focused on progress, beginnings, the overcoming of adversity. Like good teachers, we are always beginning, thinking about how to move forward from here to there. For example, our most canonical works of autoethnography (Rose; Gilyard; Villanueva), which emerged around the early 1990s and which remain foundational literacy narratives for the field, have tended to chart this most seemingly desirable course. These stories of coming into literacy, of beginning on a course of progress into which time stretches out hopefully far, have been defining for our field and, also noteworthy, largely the province of cisgendered, straight-identifying male authors. They are compelling books, a joy to teach, and yet what else might there be to explore beyond their shared narrative arcs of triumph over adversity, triumph that seems to happen despite the authors' respective differences in experience, background, theoretical influence, and writing style? These works, too, even as scholarship in the field has moved away from the genre of autoethnography (a move, I'd argue, that is fraught with its own complex tensions), have remained standards for graduate students' comprehensive reading and continue to serve as foundational, at least in terms of situating the composition classroom and the teaching of writing in the university, as a vehicle of progress.

This foundational focus on "progress," albeit an unstable term itself, coupled with a predominantly heteronormative male voice and experience, still threatens to limit our range of motion in rhetorical studies—topically, analytically, methodologically, and most importantly in terms of our ability to explore how any of these (topoi, analyses, methods), at any given time, might *make* the researcher-writer. In *Techne: Queer Meditations on Writing the Self,* Jacqueline Rhodes and Jonathan Alexander outline the goals of their multimodal project in ways that offer hopeful alternatives to more static or predictable studies of self, time, and narrative. Drawing on Gesa Kirsch and Jacqueline Jones Royster's *Feminist Rhetorical Practices,* they emphasize the potentiality of continued reflection and analysis in a digital environment:

> "Rather than distancing ourselves from the complexities of this embodied-ness, we suggest instead that we attend to it, reflect on it, observe it, and critique it and that we cultivate a stance amid the chaos of it all that enables robust inquiry." (Kirsch and Royster qtd. in Rhodes and Alexander)

In "Rhizomes," one of Rhodes's chapters within *Techne,* Rhodes discusses how Gilles Deleuze and Félix Guattari's meditation on a theory of knowledge "works with planes and interconnected and tangled lines rather than through vertical and hierarchical lines," providing a building block toward more sophisticated analysis of experience. That the rhizome "'has no beginning or end; it is always in the middle, between things, interbeing, *intermezzo,*'" allows for a kind of resistance to the linearity of traditional progress narratives. Rhodes, however, offers us a useful feminist revision of the rhizome, one that opens space for a valuing of subjective experience, of the idea of "who" or, as Rhodes notes, what Deleuze and Guattari call "'useless questions'" (qtd. in Rhodes, "Rhizomes"). For Rhodes, the search for self—which is concerned with "place and space"—steps beyond Deleuze and Guattari's conception of the rhizome as essentially "work[ing] flatly through lines rather than static point." Rhodes offers us an alternate theoretical metaphor—"rootstock"—in which "that reaching is part of an identity. Longing" ("Rhizomes"). Rhodes grounds this feminist revision in Braidotti's "nomadic subject," "a vision of subjectivity that embraces simultaneity and multiple, sometimes contradictory layers of identity" ("Rhizomes"). Explaining the rewards of this revision more fully, Rhodes writes,

The move toward the One is a narrative inclusion, the type that seeks to contain difference in order to make it legible, identifiable, and thus acceptable to a normative readership—in this case, ourselves. I would argue, however, that in our radical alterity *we are at times unknowable to ourselves*—and that it is within this incommensurability and unknowability that we find fruitful places to resist.

Here Rhodes provides essential groundwork for a researcher/writer subject that is equally searching, lost perhaps, even as we are in the process of trying to understand, to represent, to witness. Here we might find appropriate coexistence for Corder's desires for "capture" and for his inevitable vanishing, his inability to ever get it "down right."

Corder himself never fully embraces a notion of subjectivity that is multiple or shifting, though he works to examine the potentiality of a more diverse subjectivity in his later work. In "On Cancer and Freshman Composition," Corder takes up the project of understanding the incidence of cancer rhetorically as a failure of invention, a failure of our ability to allow for diversity, that "multiple and sometimes contradictory potentialities may be omnipresent within the same host" (1). He goes on to explain that perhaps we each consist of "multiple rhetorical universes" where "there is more, far more, already in us than we know, waiting to be said, waiting to find a way to be said" (3). Our failure or inability to allow for the coexistence of these "multiple rhetorical universes" within the same host causes one to overtake the other, to run rampant, cancerous. We all have this potentiality already inherent:

> We all, then, already have cancer. Cancer occurs not from an abnormal invasion, but from the normal in conflict with itself. Cancer occurs as a consequence of arrangements and congruities, or more accurately as a consequence of disarrangements and incongruities modifying otherwise normal growths. (6)

The reason for this occurrence, for Corder, is because "cells told to grow one way for twenty years cannot easily shift to another in two, and so may continue yearning toward a structure and style no longer right for their circumstances" (7).

Corder's thinking here gets lost in his word choice (the use of the word "normal") and his shift to the passive voice: "cells told to grow one way" (told by whom or what?). There is a missing agency to Corder's searching, though his intellectual investigation is important to the overall work of this book and also to the project Rhodes and Alexander pick up decades later. For Corder, the sticking point is the idea that any "one," any subjectivity, must essentially remain intact despite (or in light of) the coexistence with or experience of difference. The problem of cancer, metaphorically, in our discourse (with ourselves and with others) is "that we have not learned to let competing normalities live together in the same time and space. One must give way and be called cancer" ("On Cancer" 8). Corder's longer description of his vision exemplifies his particular sense of "yearning" toward difference:

> And that lets me think that it is possible for any of us—if the stars are right and we work to make ourselves human—to *enfold* another whose history we have not shared. In this act of enfolding, the speaker becomes through speech; the speaker's identity is always to be saved, to emerge as a compelling identity to the other, whose identity is also to be cherished. Then they may speak, each holding the other wholly in mind. Such enfolding extended, no person, no cell, no flesh is alien, and cancer vanishes. (8)

Corder seeks connection and also stability: the speaker's "identity is always to be saved," kept whole, singular. We get to be, as Newkirk muses, merely "proximate, close to," because we remain essentially whole and fully ourselves (not anyone else nor changed in the effort to explain or depict anyone else), and thus, "Perfection is a bitch and not really the right goal anyway . . . to translate someone else's words into our own, never a one-to-one transaction and often a messy one" (*Minds* 144). Here Newkirk accepts as inevitable our stable subjectivity, which essentially precludes "perfect" rendering. For his part, Corder edges into difference with the hopeful expectation that what it might yield is actually a reaffirmation of our respective subjectivities, that we remain whole even as we connect: "the speaker's identity is always to be saved, to emerge as a compelling identity to the other." When one changes the other, there has been a perversion of sorts, a cancer, which has overtaken, dominated, because "we have not learned to let competing normalities live together in the same time and space." Instead and ideally, for Corder, we are never to experience alienation, and thus never to be overtaken by cancer. All is under our control, internally and externally, already familiar.

Rhodes, in "Rhizomes," shares Corder's yearning for subjectivity, for the "long-standing feminist ethic of self-examination"—a "longing" for space and place, for rootedness—but Rhodes's revision allows for such desire to exist along "a tangled line." This revision invites, ultimately, a place to begin an exploration of subjectivity and feminist research methodology that, as Rhodes and Alexander describe their multimodal experiment in *Techne*, "leav[es] room for getting lost." Noting the human need for "stability and composure," they maintain, "We also need to make room for the kinds of writing—and the kind of subjects—that challenge such composure, that offer rich, capacious, and excessive ways of writing, reading, and experiencing." In her introduction to *Rhetorica in Motion*, Eileen Schell describes "feminist rhetorical methods and methodologies as movement, as motion, and as action," which, for Patricia Bizzell, require "'methods which violate some of the most cherished conventions of academic research, most particularly in bringing the person of the research, her body, her emotions, and dare one say, her soul into the work'" (qtd. in Schell and Rawson 4–6). Building on Rhodes and Alexander here, we might add that the "person of the research" might be *both* researcher and participant, or perhaps even multiple, complex, and entwined subjectivities of each. For Rhodes, to work from such subjective, searching positionalities ensures that we might become "at times unknowable to ourselves" ("Rhizomes").

I offer up this book as one humble model, my own rendering, of what Rhodes and Alexander describe. Given that the dialogue Sue and I shared was shaped by terminal illness and her experience of the body in its decline, the temporal locus is "out of step" in ways that squarely refuse the traditional "progress narrative," its normativity and predictability. Extending the rhizome's temporal location in the "middle," I argue that we might also take up *endings* as a space for reinvigorating our conversations, for looping back into complexity and investigation into what we might learn in the aftermath of our losses, our endings. Rather than one man acting on and through and even despite his environment, I am one woman writing here out of the experience of being part of "two," ever-influenced by and still internally, intellectually, in dialogue with Susan Lundy Maute. This book examines the function of language, of words—written and spoken—in a collaborative effort to understand, come to, or even achieve dying, and in so doing I offer up a failed writer, the one who remains. I am an impossible, imperfect, incomplete subject. Together we worked on an island of sorts, a communicative space we shared with each other, in order to contend with breast cancer in its last throes. This is not, however, a study of breast cancer narratives, though such work is emergent and I think compelling in rhetorical studies; Sue's "breast cancer story" is not mine to tell in any succinct or comprehensive way.[10] Further, my move to refer to myself now as "one" and previously "of two" is made while taking up consciously the challenge posited by Rhodes and Alexander. My hope is that I might offer some investigation of the dividing, destabilized, and ever-evolving subjectivity that I occupy now as researcher-writer-friend, as the "one" left behind, and also of our collaborative identity, our existence as a partnership in the search for meaning and for intellectual and emotional foothold amid the progression of Sue's illness. I find Corder's "rhetorical cancer" compelling and, rather than take comfort in avoiding it as he hopes, ask: How might the loss of control, of being somehow overtaken, teach us about what we do—and who we might be—as researchers and writers? Why might movement into uncertainty and loss function as yet another rich brand of knowledge making?

While I will give more attention to scholarship in rhetorics of disability later in this book, I want to link my project, and particularly this consideration of our partnership in the midst of great physical difference, to Stephanie Kerschbaum's approach to difference as "dynamic, relational, and emergent" (57). In *Toward a New Rhetoric of Difference*, Kerschbaum offers an exemplifying critique of Anne Jurecic's discussion of a student—Gregory—whom Jurecic identifies, after an assessment of his characteristics via her own independent research, as having Asperger's syndrome. In her move to "diagnose" Gregory, which is, on the surface, an effort to "help students like Gregory and teachers working with students like Gregory," Jurecic also problematically "fixes—that is, freezes—autism-as-difference" (Kerschbaum 60). For Kerschbaum, the project at hand ought to be instead "to engage a dialectic between stasis and motion, between fixity and change" (64). Drawing on Mikhail Bakhtin, Kerschbaum seeks a definition of difference "predicated upon . . . separateness," where we might think of "the shaping of difference interactionally" (67).

Just as Kerschbaum's work affirms that we pay attention to subjectivity, a call shared with Corder and Rhodes, she also creates a kind of space in which a pair, "learning with" each other interactionally amid difference, might carve out a wholly unique experience. This allows, I would argue, for the kind of foundational transport Rhodes describes, where we might indeed become "unknowable" to ourselves. Kerschbaum writes, again noting Bakhtin, "No two individuals will ever have the same relation to each other as they do to any other individual, and no situation will be exactly like any other current, past, or future situation" (68). Kerschbaum here makes a call for nuance, for attention to detail and particularity, the sort of which affirms not only the value of the "small-scale" study, which this book takes up, but also the expectation of a shifting, unstable subjectivity that is temporal and experiential. That we might move in and out of these enclosed interactions, moving from one to two and then from two to one, suggests too that we might ourselves shift and expand with each interaction. This book asks that we consider the research-writer in motion: that we might continuously and cumulatively change and transgress as we move across time and experience; in the richest moments, we may become unrecognizable to ourselves.

While I expect (and hope) that Rhodes and Alexander's thinking will continue to inform work in the field more broadly, I would argue that we have yet to realize or at least to boldly experiment with—*to queer*—our research methodologies and our researcher-subjectivities, and that is despite foundational work by scholars like Kirsch and Royster, Schell, Bizzell, and others, work that calls for a reflexivity of the sort aligned with Rhodes and Alexander's conceptual project.[11] In part, I believe some of this has to do with disciplinary chasms that differentiate sharply qualitative, social science–based research from more humanities-based research. Additionally, I would argue that we tend to avert our analytical gaze in many cases away from ourselves and understandably toward our students or participants.[12] We may end with the sweeping, "And so now how do I teach this?" or "What can we learn about the teaching of writing given Study X?" Surely such a move is one I've employed in my own work as well. The classroom first brought me into the field and will forever keep my attention and imagination. However, my call here is that we additionally make some self-conscious room for the playing out of our own "unknowableness," our own experience of becoming lost as an element of study and method. I believe such attentiveness will ultimately stretch and reinvent not only our scholarly work but also our teaching.

While I will return to this piece later in this book, I want to highlight here as foundational Peter Smagorinsky's much-acclaimed essay "The Method Section as Conceptual Epicenter in Constructing Social Science Research Reports." With a traditional "IMRaD" format ("Introduction, Methods, Results, and Discussion") as a point of reference, Smagorinsky laments the many poorly executed studies he has reviewed over the years and isolates their roots as such:

> Authors go awry when they either pose no research questions, or pose different questions at different points in the manuscript, or pose questions that are not answerable through the data, or pose answerable questions but present results that appear unrelated to the questions. In my experience, studies work best when an author poses a limited set of answerable questions and then designs the paper around them. (405)

While an IMRaD format was never my planned framework, I did draw on qualitative methods of data collection in my work with Sue—recorded interviews and transcription, surveys—and one of the hallmarks of our collaboration was our continual slippage into exactly the kinds of questions Smagorinsky warns of, "different questions at different points . . . or . . . questions that are not answerable through the data." As time went on and as Sue's illness progressed, our conversation routinely pursued the unknowable: the questions we posed to each other were often unanswerable, and such ambiguity functions here as an analytical "conclusion" of sorts.[13] While this dynamic and the kind of analysis it ultimately engenders—one that uses qualitative methods to create essentially "primary source texts" that we can then read as scholars trained in the humanities—compose a theme for this book, I think it key that we confront the limits posed by Smagorinsky's claims and see them as an opportunity for productive divergence and also for a hearkening back (should we have drifted a bit) into the kind of feminist inquiry that may confound more than it clarifies. On one hand, it is important to fairly contextualize Smagorinsky's advice: in fact, traditionally practiced social scientific analysis tends to benefit from adherence to such standards. As I work out of a feminist tradition in rhetoric-composition, a field often betwixt and between, with roots in both the humanities and the social sciences, I wonder what more deliberate, reflective divergence from Smagorinsky's lines might evoke in our qualitative work? How much room might we have for boundary crossing, for blurring more openly, more directly, our scholarly existence as "in between," *intermezzo*, as Rhodes's adaption of the rhizome celebrates so well?

While this book owes a debt to work in medical rhetorics and also medical anthropology (Wells; Barton; Mattingly and Garro), which investigates the functioning of medical language, spoken and written, in constructing both patients' and doctors' experience of illness and its treatment, it also takes as a model Rita Charon's foundational work in narrative medicine. Charon, trained as both a medical doctor and a literary scholar, is primarily responsible for a disciplinary area devoted to the merger of medicine, treatment and diagnosis, and narrativity. Charon describes her work of teaching medical clinicians to listen for, understand, and appreciate narrative structure in their patients' communications as follows:

> I am trying to strengthen those cognitive and imaginative abilities that are required for one person to take in and appreciate the

representation—and therefore the reality—of another. Whether that representation is in visual art, a fictional text, or the spoken words of a patient in the office, the one who absorbs and *confirms* the representation must have the capacities to witness and give meaning to the situation as depicted. Only then can its receiver be moved to act on behalf of its creator. (113)

Charon's linking of listening and expression with, ultimately, clinical action is a complex blending of medical expertise and empathy, a combination uniquely under strain given today's challenges to health care. It also opens up both patients and their doctors to a kind of personal expression that parallels much of the desire we can trace in expressivist scholarship in rhetoric-composition, filled with the conviction that the ability to articulate or witness something uniquely personal drives the best kind of practice, the best kind of writing instruction and student learning.

Charon's call for attention to patients' unique communications and constructed realities relies on a disrupted or dislocated relationship to temporality. This hints of Rhodes's "rootstock": *intermezzo* or, at least, out of step with time while also "longing for place or space" (Rhodes, "Rhizomes"). Charon explains her project:

The seriously ill people for whom we care in clinical practice are marooned between stable states. They are no longer defined by work role, family role, or state role and not yet defined as simply awaiting death but de-differentiated by cotton hospital gowns and plastic wristbands to be side by side only with others who, too, find themselves in the limbo regions of sickness. And those of us who have elected to live our lives with the sick must "wholly attend," must be *with* them, must open ourselves to porous transit on their journeys while building collectives of our own that help to get the work done. (220)

While Charon's ending sentiment here is one of practical application—"to get the work done"—the possibility for "porous transit" suggests a set of key opportunities crucial to the work of this book. First, Charon's "porous transit" allows for impact: patient to doctor and doctor to patient. In taking in another's journey, we might indeed become, as Rhodes notes, "unknowable to ourselves," and we might, too, move along a continuum of practice. This means that, in occupying a space with patients that is set *outside* all the predictable roles and rhythms both doctors and patients are accustomed to, doctors may find new ways of "getting the work done" from places that are alternate, removed, unpredictable, and in fact better aligned with patient needs.

I take up a similar project in this book in the context of feminist rhetorical studies. Rhetoric-composition scholars/researchers/writers are practitioners of a discipline that handles, that indeed works by hand with, language, and I wonder how we too might *get the work done* if some of that work involves (is made of) our own porousness, how the motivation and push *for the work*—our research participants/collaborators and their pain, their stories, their sometimes fraught, twisted relationship to words—might be taken in as part of our very work.[14] How far might we be flung conceptually and materially? If we find a way back into, as Rhodes seeks, "place or space," what might these look like and why? How might our newly found spaces/places be different from what we knew before? In what ways might we use our own porousness as an agent of knowledge making and a vehicle for becoming new kinds of writers and researchers? Why begin to work out of step, dislocated, in between, searching, lost? While postmodern theory has given much to examination of such questions—informing work in autoethnography (a particularly notable example is Victor Villanueva's *Bootstraps*) and multimodal and digital rhetorics (for which Rhodes and Alexander's work is exemplary)—I balk at categorizing this work squarely along postmodern lines. Instead I work always in contact with the body dying, and this necessitates that we return again and again to these questions: What are we doing and why? How are our bodies (data, texts, organs) failing us? And what can we learn at the pressure points? I would argue that we have not carved out a comparable practice in rhetorical analyses for our handling of qualitative data, nor have we managed, really, to blend qualitative work with other, perhaps more flexible and unpredictable genres. My hope is that this book might serve as one model for such experimentation in ways that invite others to seek out and try their own modes.

A Call for Meaning

If you die like an athlete, it means that you die on the field. You die knowing the time is running out, knowing the clock is ticking, knowing the chances are slimming and slimming. But you die dirty and sweaty. You show integrity and lean into it until the last minute. You push your teammates until the end. Not until the whistle blows, until time is done, is the game lost. (Restaino, "Reflection: Athlete")

At its core, the book takes as its guiding push Susan Lundy Maute's struggle and triumph through terminal illness and her decision to take me inside that experience in profoundly personal ways. We shared a desire to understand things that felt out of our respective grasps, and I'd venture a guess that some of what drove that striving, particularly in light of that which was ultimately inexplicable, was our shared athleticism. Athletes routinely experience and even celebrate striving and falling short, pushing the body to its limits to see merely how far it can go and knowing fully that in this pushing they will find their end point. For Sue, living with terminal illness operated similarly, and that there was an end point—coming to terms with her own death—functioned much as the athlete in the last seconds of a losing competition: inevitable but somehow also meaningful, honorable if played out fully. This is a notion I have long understood in its athletic context, but it marks new ground for me as a thinker, writer, and researcher. How might failure, endings, loss give us new places and spaces from which to work, to go forward?

Sue wrote a short piece, "Hello Cancer," which serves as the "Bloodwork" entry before this chapter. In it, she addresses her illness as a kind of personified foe while considering, alternately, that cancer might be instead a teacher, an ally with secrets for living and growth. Expressing her hope for some value, some promise that all will not be for naught, she explains,

> I hate the thought of having my life cut short by something I have no control over and that I don't understand. . . . My biggest worry, however, is that the effort put forth to overcome these challenges will not really matter in the end; that they are not life lessons.

This idea of "life lessons" resonates with what I see as a central concern of this book: academic work—research and writing—as bound up in living, as part of our human growth. Coming to terms, claiming her own death, ultimately became, for Sue, a way of stepping beyond this worry, of conquering her situation and assigning meaning despite her inevitable death. Our collaboration remains a rhetorical space (sacred to me) in which she—with me, taking me—did the thinking, writing, and talking work necessary to achieve such authority over the untimely end of her life. In exposing my own movement through an experience that was at once intellectual and emotional, I hope this book might serve as a testament to intimate human struggle as methodological and to the capacity of feminist rhetorical practices in allowing and generating spaces in which transformation can occur. Such transformation, when we use the frame of terminal illness as a lens for reading, marks a way to render ourselves as writing and thinking subjects and to subsequently destabilize the texts we produce. Making room for this work in the field, inviting others to build on what they might find here, is my effort to honor the many gifts she gave me, including the blessing for this book, and—in so doing—I hold Susan Lundy Maute as my constant collaborator even as I now write alone.

BLOODWORK
(AN INTERVIEW TRANSCRIPT)

This interview transcript comes from a conversation I had with Sue on 24 March 2014.

SUE: Yeah. Well the thing about this, which we've talked about in the past, is the surrender piece.

JESSICA: Um, for the record, funny you should say that . . . the tentative . . . the book proposal that I wrote was tentatively titled Surrender *. . .*

S: 'Cause that's what it's really . . .

J: —and for me too, from a researcher perspective . . . it's like kind of like you set out, because that's just how you're taught to learn certain things and ask certain questions. And then there's a point where, okay, if you're going to learn more you're going to let go of your agenda and just be like . . .

S: Right. Any preconceived notions . . . let go of the outcome.

J: Exactly. All of a sudden I find myself asking questions that neither you nor I can answer. Or find myself . . . or . . . another thing that's really changed, that is different than in my world, is like there's certain things that I can't figure out without you. Like I feel like I need to be in conversation with you to figure these things out. Like especially the stuff about collaboration and that kind of thing that's an interesting piece to all of this stuff. So in other words it's like I can't . . . I transcribe these . . . and I sit and I listen to you and type it all out . . .

S: Oh wow. That's impressive.

J: So I listen . . . and I can type pretty fast . . . but it's always good when you burst out laughing, because it gives me some extra time to catch up.

S: [laughing]

J: I still have hours of transcription work to do but I've done a lot. But anyway . . . the process is you take all your data, you transcribe all these interviews, you take all your artifacts, you know the written texts and the everything . . . and then you figure out . . . what do I have here? But what does it mean to say, well, I can't figure this out by myself. I have all this stuff but I can't really even figure it all out by myself. So it's like—here—

S: For you to do— *[silly/laughing]*

J: What the hell am I supposed to do with this shit? [laughing]

STAGE III
ROOTING SURRENDER
RHYTHM, DISSONANCE, AND LETTING GO IN THE RESEARCH PROCESS

> The experience of thirdness is akin to following a shared theme in musical improvisation. The third which both partners follow is a rhythmic structure or pattern that both simultaneously create and surrender to. Such cocreation is like transitional experience in having the paradoxical quality of being invented and discovered. To the question, "Who created this rhythm, you or I?" the paradoxical answer, both and neither. It is impossible and unnecessary to say who has created the pattern because, unlike in verbal speech, in music and dance we can receive and transmit information at the same time. (Benjamin, "Intersubjectivity, Thirdness" 13)

In her extensive work in feminist psychoanalytic theory, Jessica Benjamin writes often of the importance of "surrender" to "thirdness." Over decades, Benjamin has ventured many eloquent attempts at defining her version of the "third"—"felt as mental space to negotiate meaning"—and also of the correlative, necessary act of surrender, which operates itself with rhythmicity, following threads of connection ("Intersubjectivity, Thirdness" 2). While neither term originates exclusively with Benjamin, her writing on "intersubjectivity"—which finds its roots most formally in her 1988 *Bonds of Love*—is perhaps one of her great contributions to feminist theory and a key concept through which to enact both thirdness and surrender.[1] For Benjamin, who seeks in *Bonds* to "adopt a feminist critique of gender polarity" and also an analysis of submission, intersubjectivity operates as the "tension between interacting individuals rather than that within the individual" (29). It also resists, most crucially, "complementarity," which she defines as the "push-me-pull-you, doer-done to dynamics we find in most impasses" (2). It's here, in traditional complementary relations, that we break down into an "either/or" reductive binary exchange. While Benjamin explores how this dynamic plays out in the context of the psychotherapeutic relationship, in fact I find Benjamin's model a valuable frame for understanding both the possibilities inherent in doing collaborative, feminist research and writing in rhetorical studies, particularly when we pursue projects (and topics) that exceed our easy control, and our more formalized or familiar tools for analysis, research, and writing. Working within Benjamin's frame, I ask: When we resist complementary relationships with research collaborators, what might our dynamic look like? What is an intersubjective research collaboration, and why is it valuable for work in feminist rhetorical studies? How might we rethink the loss of our expected, more structured dynamics—those complementary relations and roles—while also embracing an emerging if unfamiliar rhythm? Who is the emerging researcher in such a dynamic? Building on Benjamin, what does it mean for the researcher to "surrender" into a process, a collaborative endeavor, or a topic (in the case of this work, terminal illness)? What are some of the possible outcomes in how we do our work, how we write and learn to make sense of different kinds of data? My goal in this chapter is to establish a terminological basis from which to ultimately explore these questions about who we can become and how this becoming might alter the sorts of knowledge we make.

While the contemporary mind may flash an image of a white flag upon hearing the word "surrender," in fact its roots—in the Latin *reddere* (to return) and *rendere* (to render)—find alternate, historical literary uses in Pope, Milton, Shakespeare, and Dryden, among others.[2] While my project here is not to offer analyses of these works, situating the term in its historical context opens a pathway for its use in this book and certainly in Benjamin's theoretical frame. On a basic level, the roots of the word do not denote a "giving up," the sort we imagine on the battlefield, but rather a kind of reciprocal return, "to give in return, to make return of" (*Oxford*). In Pope's *Iliad* translation, we see the function of the root word clearly: "Till Helen's woes at full reveng'd appear, / And Troy's proud matrons render tear for tear" (11.324). "Render," as it functions here, is an act of mirroring: each of Helen's tears is matched or returned in equal measure by "Troy's proud matrons." Perhaps Shakespeare's *Troilus and Cressida* offers us the fullest use of the root, particularly given the relational exchange here with "others," the depiction of self-knowledge via applause:

> No man is lord of anything,
> Though in and of him there be much consisting,
> Till he communicate his parts to others:
> Nor doth he of himself know them for aught
> Till he behold them formed in the applause
> Where they're extended: which like an arch, reverberates
> The voice again; or, like a gate of steel
> Fronting the sun, receives and renders back
> His figure and his heat.   (III, iii, 11115–122)

Shakespeare's play exposes for us the perils of identity—its dependency on public consumption or validation—a phenomenon long-explored in rhetorical studies via theories of audience, and one we see as a kind of preoccupation around the personal in Corder and later in Newkirk (as discussed in the previous chapter). Fundamentally, and for better or for worse, we come to know something of ourselves as "rendered" back: we appear; we discover or interpret our own impact or energy in relational terms. We are vulnerable to the exploits of translation and the instability of human relationship.

Extending, then, this idea of "surrender" as Benjamin imagines it and as the word's historical roots suggest, I understand the concept along the lines of relational exchange, shared motion, a phenomenon of contact and mutual impact after we are changed in some way. This is not without risk: we risk confrontation with our own mess of longing and need, our own searching and capacity for loss. My experience as Sue's journey partner, recorder of many of her fears and wishes, came with costs, my own loss and sense of isolation among them. In the last weeks of her life, Sue suffered from a scary internal bleed. This is a story I will return to and reconsider from multiple standpoints later in the book. For my purposes here, I will fast forward to the aftermath of the bleed when I showed up at the hospital to take Sue home. I knew she would be shaken by the prospect of leaving the security of the hospital, and indeed I found her sad and contemplative. I wrote the following reflection, remembering our exchange later that night, and particularly Sue's efforts to praise my role:

> I sat on the edge of the bed and we were instantly in a place together,
> an island of a kind, the one that I can't seem to fully describe to

anyone or fully share. You were sad and reflective, quiet, and I knew you'd be worried about going home. We don't have to rush, I thought. There's no rush.

"I was always someone, growing up, who always looked to other people, looked at other people and thought—wow—*that person is so amazing, so impressive.* I never thought, never thought of myself . . . but you, . . . I am so grateful to you because you have shown me myself. . . ."

I started to cry a bit, to try to tell you that it's mutual, that you've given me *my religion* of sneakers and the body and outside and movement. I've done some crying for you this week, I confessed to you. I don't want you to worry about me. I don't need you to worry about me.

"Just as a friend, you know . . ."

You're not taking care of me. But you are taking care of me, constantly. What am I going to do, that this person—that you—are one of the orbits around which I understand things about life, what makes it good and also what makes it so dark and heavy? Where am I supposed to go from here with all that you have taught and shown me? (Restaino, "Reflection: Week of 7/7/14")

I quote this excerpt at length with both hesitancy and humility. I hesitate because the memory of this exchange is so very dear to me that my impulse is to keep it private, all to myself. And I find the sharing of this exchange humbling since I know that Sue's claim about what I was doing for her—*you have shown me myself*—was far beyond my deliberate control or awareness; nor was it evidence of shining character on my part. I am in fact far less worthy of praise or accolades than I might appear in Sue's rendering of me, her attempt to express her gratitude and her valuing of our collaboration at a moment of great vulnerability in her illness. My agency, I would instead argue, was perpetually in a state of slippage or shift: in praising me, Sue is not in fact revealing who I was then independently, or had always been. Rather, our dynamic continued to remake me. As I served as her witness, her recorder, her scribe, the keeper of her thoughts and narrative, I was both rendered anew within our dynamic while also reoriented to my own body and mind. As I write this book, this rendering continues to unfold. We exist in a kind of perpetual motion together, and, in fact, I continue to watch the evolution over time.

Thus the experience of "surrender," at least according to its historical, etymological roots, does not operate along complementary (doer/

done to) lines, as with contemporary associations with the term. In her lecture "Intersubjectivity, Thirdness, and Mutual Recognition," Benjamin explains, "Surrender is not To Someone . . . giving in or over to someone, an idealized person or thing" (2). When we have indeed submitted to another, according to Benjamin, we experience "the felt absence of freedom to explore and discuss the meaning of what has just happened" (6). In contrast, the space in which we might in fact "explore . . . what has just happened" between us is Benjamin's "third," a space that "begins with the early non-verbal experience of sharing a pattern, a dance, with another person" and that opens room for "being able to connect with the other's mind while accepting her separateness and difference" (7, 2). This is the arena for Benjamin's surrender: rhythmic, vulnerable, unpredictable, and collaborative. While not a space dedicated to domination, it is surely one tinged with loss. For no sooner are we able to emerge or exist in unique relation to another than the stakes heighten, our capacities shift. In my case, my apprehension—at once recognition of what I had and what I would ultimately lose—is written into the last line of my reflection: "Where am I supposed to go from here with all that you have taught and shown me?"

The loss I anticipate with such anxiety in my journal entry is in part a material one, as Sue's physical decline was immediately evident at the time of that writing, creating a space between us that would silence our talk and halt our exchange of texts. In rhetorical studies, Debra Hawhee's efforts to explore the historical roots of rhetoric as an art of "the body as well as the mind" parallel Benjamin's claims about rhythmicity ("Bodily Pedagogies" 144).[3] In her examination of the interrelatedness of classical athletic and rhetorical training, Hawhee isolates "the three Rs . . . rhythm, repetition, and response" (145). Most notable is the extent to which these three factors ensure both structure and unpredictability concurrently. Hawhee explains through analogy,

> It is the interrelation between the generalized path of the riverbed with its interruptive rocks and sediment on the one hand, and the force of the water's current on the other, that produces the eddies and swirls, the sudden shifts in direction within the general flow—herein lies the rhythm. Rhythm therefore produces distinctive movements within a generalized direction; it combines fixity with variability. (148)

For Hawhee, athletes engage in this rhythmic tension in competition. Examining the blending of athletic and rhetorical education in an ancient wrestling manual, Hawhee writes,

The opponent's moves and the attention to specificity they require introduce difference to the repetition, demanding a new move in between each of the throwing directives. Stylistically, the manual captures the difference between repetitions, demanding and producing its own kind of rhythmic response. (149)

The demand for "response" suggests that the rhythm, for Hawhee, is driven by the actors involved, those players who must, in Benjamin's rendering, be "able to connect with the other's mind while accepting her separateness and difference" (Benjamin, "Intersubjectivity, Thirdness" 2). In Benjamin's conceptualization of surrender—at least for the sake of maintaining the rhythm or the "dance" itself—*neither* player succumbs "to" the other. If she does, the rhythm is lost and domination, complementarity occurs. For Hawhee's wrestlers, this means victory for one and defeat for the other. Terminal illness upends our familiar rhythms and asks us to learn a new way of being, to contend with the threat of domination, and to perhaps also rethink it.

In many pursuits, wrestling one of them, domination is the ultimate goal. But this end goal represents, for Benjamin, submission rather than surrender. Attempting to describe surrender as she experiences it in the writing process, Benjamin—like Hawhee—draws on the metaphor of a running current:

The process of writing has something to do with faith in desire, in the process of following a thread, swimming along with the current. This process has everything to do with "the area of faith" as Eigen (1981) called it. . . . Without surrendering to a process of open discovery, to acceptance of the unknown, how can we not be doomed to mere repetition? ("From Many Into One" 196)

We might think of this "open discovery" and resistance to "mere repetition" as inherent in any rhythmic process between equals, as Hawhee notes: "The sudden shifts in direction within the general flow—herein lies the rhythm." Of course, unique to terminal illness is a rhythm marked by both unpredictability and inevitability. On one hand, the day-to-day process of living with terminal illness seems rife with "shifts in direction," good days and some very bad days. But as bad days increasingly make up most of the week, the dance and the rhythm seem to pick up at an increasingly predictable pace. At the same time, at the end of this dance, to draw on Michael Eigen, is the ultimate challenge of "acceptance of the unknown," the vast space occupied by dying and the extraordinary experience of loss. Such loss, too, occurs in the context of the dynamic between us, and in this particular exchange, we at once lose the long-valued opportunity to discuss, as Benjamin writes, "what has just happened" and—as our relational dance halts—we each exist as vulnerable to domination: Sue in my rendering of her, of us, of what happened, and me in "doing" method, text, and grief now alone. In my case, all of these were cocreated in our intersubjective dynamic—grief, too, as we mourned her death together before she was gone—and to go them alone is for me a foreign territory of sorts, a new process entirely, since the work itself was shaped by the currents of our living dynamic.

While we can imagine the idea of "following a thread" and a kind of rhythmic tension in our collaborations with others, there is great risk involved in following that very thread into new discoveries about who we might be and what kind of knowledge we might produce. Furthermore, to the extent that what we gain seems valuable—for all kinds of reasons—surrender comes with the looming threat, the likelihood, in fact, that we will arrive one day at the very end of our beloved string. Accordingly, I ask: What does it mean to work from a place of loss, or at least with or amid the threat of loss? What might we create and build on the other side, moving into and working out of those spaces that render us uncertain or scared or weak in ways we had not been before? Understandably, we often resist such experiences. However, "surrender" of the sort Benjamin imagines does not operate as an oppositional binary to such resistance. Emmanuel Ghent, longtime mentor to Benjamin, insists that "surrender might be thought of as reflective of some 'force' towards growth" and "is not a voluntary activity. One cannot choose to surrender, though one can choose to submit. One can provide facilitative conditions for surrender but cannot make it happen" (109). In Ghent's construction, "resistance" and "submission" halt the drive toward growth and are efforts to maintain what is familiar, known, recognizable, and thus not frightening. While Benjamin insists that surrender is never "to" another, Ghent also underscores an absence of control: embedded here is a kind of impossible agency of the sort I tried to describe in my experience of Sue's valuing of our collaboration. In fact I could not make her see herself in any particular way, nor could she do that for me. Rather, we were—and I would argue I continue to be, though differently now—each in process with the other so that each was remade over and over again. This results in a kind of contradictory tension, a kind of dependency and mutual impact that is not simply about depletion or domination but that is certainly about being changed in ways that can feel overwhelming and intimidating. Ghent describes these characteristics of the experience of surrender: "dread and death, and/or clarity, relief, even ecstasy" (109). In such relational dynamics we also, according to Ghent, surpass or transcend time: "being 'in the moment,' totally in the present, where past and future, the two tenses that require 'mind' in the sense of secondary processes, have receded from consciousness" (109). We neither rescue time nor shape it, and we are free—at least for a frozen moment—to move experientially rather than through a deliberative series of planned steps with a visible end goal.

While the quality of straddling time harks back to the longings of both Corder and Newkirk in their calls for writing from a personal narrative stance and their claims for a subjectivity that freezes a moment via the author's recounting, both also craft a subjectivity that hints of submissiveness over surrender, at least as Ghent describes the term. While for Ghent self-discovery is perhaps the most profound characteristic of surrender, he writes that this experience is "quite unlike submission in which the reverse happens: one feels one's self as a puppet in the power of another; one's sense of identity atrophies" (109). Conversely, and as discussed in the last chapter, Newkirk's clear valuing of and search for a subjectivity happens anxiously through his audience ("are you still there?"), clearly staking out the terms of his desire: "I want you to believe that 'I am with you and know how it is'" (*Minds* 18). Newkirk's revelation here strikes me as a human impulse for recognition and yet notably aligned with Ghent's characteristics of submission as a search for self where power is in the other, where "one's sense of identity atrophies" (Ghent 109). Notable here too is that for Newkirk, the move into personal narrative is an effort to control or assign some structure to time—"history is the form we give to time"—for the purpose of "explanation, meaning, self-understanding" (*Minds* 145). Corder's approach is different but equally in contrast to Ghent. Though Corder insists, comparatively, that we have no control over time, his impulse for self-revelation nevertheless seeks control: "Since we don't have time, we must rescue time by putting it into our discourses and holding it there" ("Argument as Emergence" 31). Terminal illness, and indeed many such experiences that show us our own smallness, renders traditional notions of heroism and rescue impossible. Yet without the prospect of an answer or a solution, we may move productively, meaningfully into the darkness. My work here to define terminology is an effort to construct ways of thinking about such moves that underscore a kind of generative potential for rhetorical work. When there is indeed "nothing to say" or even to do to reverse, rescue, or cure, what is the role of rhetoric?

While this book attempts to model a way of working and creating that offers one response to this question about rhetoric in such a dark space, I want to resist falling into the complementary, binary patterns that Benjamin warns against. Accordingly, some sort of middle ground that values our situatedness in, even our attachments to, audience, time, and our emerging subjectivit(ies) while also making room for the unknown and unpredictable is key. Returning again to "Rhizomes," a chapter from Jacqueline Rhodes and Jonathan Alexander's collaborative digital work, *Techne: Queer Meditations on Writing the Self*, Rhodes theorizes knowledge making that combines timelessness and a desire for "place and space," or stability and self. Building on Deleuze and Guattari's model for knowledge, the rhizome, which "'has no beginning or end; it is always in the middle, between things, interbeing, *intermezzo*,'" Rhodes gives us the feminist revision, the metaphorical "rootstock" in which "that reaching is part of an identity. Longing." In Rhodes's formulation, knowledge is made both through "rootedness" in place and time while simultaneously allowing for changeability and contradiction. This conceptual mix of stability and unpredictability guarantees a kind of slipperiness or evasiveness to our efforts to create knowledge, to understand and to write ourselves or others. Reaching "intermezzo" may render us, again, "unknowable to ourselves." The experience of becoming in fact more lost, a process of self-discovery that Rhodes argues is uniquely queer, suggests that failure is an inseparable, inherent part of complex forms of knowledge making. And in this formulation, Newkirk's anxiety about "keeping" his audience is thus well-founded: we are, at least in part, meant to lose.

Jack Halberstam's 2011 *The Queer Art of Failure* informs Rhodes and Alexander's collaborative project in *Techne* with its insistence on the meaning-making, activist-inspired slant of failure, loss, and "unbecoming" (Halberstam 2). While the analytical focus of Halberstam's book is popular culture, the central argument is one relevant across disciplinary hegemonies and warns against academics' tendencies toward universalizing method, genre, text, and process in how we do our work. According to Halberstam, "Under certain circumstances failing, losing, forgetting, unmaking, undoing, unbecoming, not knowing may in fact offer more creative, more cooperative, more surprising ways of being in the world" (2). Drawing on Foucault, Halberstam calls for "'a theoretical production that does not need a visa from some common regime to establish its validity'" (10). It is in failing, letting go, being essentially disciplinarily disobedient in our work that we might ultimately find spaces for the new, for invention, and also for subversion. Halberstam's discussion of feminist approaches to "negativity" and "radical passivity" exemplifies resistance at the heart of thoughtful, deliberate failures. Invoking Spivak, Halberstam explains:

> Spivak's call for a "female intellectual" who does not disown another version of womanhood, femininity, and feminism, indeed for any kind of intellectual who can learn how not to know the other, how not to sacrifice the other on behalf of his or her own sovereignty, is a call that has largely gone unanswered. It is this version of feminism that I seek to inhabit, a feminism that fails to save others or to replicate itself, a feminism that finds purpose in its own failure. (128)

In my collaboration with Sue, the impossibility of "saving" took on both practical and conceptual meanings, as I could not save her from dying—no one could—nor can I presently save or even replicate her through textual representation in our work following her death. My writing about our collaboration now is thus always driven forward as much by what it can do as by what it cannot do. As a researcher and writer, I work from a place of anticipated loss—which can be traced through much of my primary source materials or the data generated in this work—and from actual loss, the eventual, inevitable end point of the work. I ask: What uniquely is made there and how can we learn about language, text, and words and how we use them? Why is there rhetorical value in the unknowable?

Halberstam's "failed" feminism provides an essential thread for this book and offers some useful response to these questions, particularly as I must explore my own unraveling as a researcher and writer, my loss of a more formalized research methodology, my increasing inability to separate the personal from the professional, the emotional from the intellectual, and—ultimately—the profound, real loss of my collaborator, my friend, in ways that have forced me to write this book alone and through an awareness of the holes and inadequacies in my own remembering and experience. I am now the only one left to render the story of our collaboration, to make an argument for its potential value to how we write and do research in feminist rhetorical studies. There is thus an extent to which this rendering, this arguing, must be laced, consistently, with failure, with reminders of its very shortcomings. In my efforts to enact this work I expect to operate consistently across, to model even, the contradictions inherent in calls for subjectivity and the personal, for clear, reproducible methods, for terminology that is static and generalizable.

As failure and loss undergird this project, its theoretical frame should be consistently held at bay. In other words, my efforts in this chapter to operationalize the term "surrender" are, of course, complex and contradictory. I have attempted to assign authority and meaning to root uses of the word via the *OED* (and canonical, largely masculinist texts) while simultaneously linking this root usage to the work of Jessica Benjamin, a feminist psychoanalytic thinker, and her mentor Emmanuel Ghent, who, despite his significance to psychoanalytic thought, is most well known for his work as a musical composer.[4] While the central bent of Benjamin's articulation of intersubjectivity and surrender is a resistance to reductive, binary relations, to domination and submission, in fact Ghent's very efforts to categorize surrender as opposed to submission tend to reinscribe these very binaries. There are strict rules to surrender, for Ghent: it's never voluntary; it's always self-defining; it pursues wholeness and unity (in self and with others); it resists or undoes fragmentation. In fact it is hard to imagine that, should we ultimately surrender in the ways Benjamin describes, where we are indeed able to "connect with the other's mind while accepting her separateness and difference," we might still (or newly) emerge "whole" as Ghent insists (2). It seems reasonable to argue instead that what we might find in Benjamin's "third" is our own undoing, as Halberstam might predict, our very "unbecoming" where in rhythm with another we lose ourselves, become in fact mysteries to ourselves. While I think this outcome is not necessarily contradicted by Benjamin's work, surely in Ghent's this tension is clearly evident. We are thus charged with the task of writing and doing research into the unknown, amid contradiction and toward failure, toward our own loss.

As rhetorical study has never been grounded in pure science, despite a handful of famously failed attempts otherwise, the consequences for this book's honest embrace of failure are multiple, diverse, and I think entirely appropriate. I see myself as alternately surrendering into the work as Benjamin describes it, following its threads, stepping in and out of the rhythms engendered by our collaboration, and yet, at times *also* submitting to it. This submission is about the power the project has had over me, the ways in which the collaboration has forced me to unlearn method, to grieve, to lose, to accept my very inadequacies as the one who remains. In practice, these qualities of surrender and submission manifest themselves in a few key ways in this book: through real loss rendered in words, as Sue and I ultimately sought a rhetoric for dying; in resistance to predictable, totalizing narratives; in a failure of more formalized, sanctioned, orderly research methods and academic genre; and in a failure of a singular or whole subjectivity in my role as writer/researcher/friend, as these roles are not just incomplete but also at times in conflict with each other. Resisting the rules of Benjamin's third at least somewhat, my hope is that I might also be able to explore "what happened" in my moments of loss, of being dominated by this work; even still, I concede at least partially to Benjamin's claims about the impossibility of critical reflection amid domination. In fact, I expect that aspects of my own loss and failure may at times exceed my linguistic grasp on these pages.

Dying as Failure, Failure as Hope

There is more written on the experience of death—in literature but also in the social sciences—than this book could ever adequately or comprehensively take on. Still, I want to root my consideration of the dying process in the foundational work of Elisabeth Kübler-Ross, whose 1969 psychological study, *On Death and Dying*, illuminated the experiences of the dying in profoundly new ways. For Kübler-Ross, countless interviews with terminally ill patients underscored the importance of communication around and about death; doctors, she argues, must engage the issue in a spirit of compassionate honesty. What seems so inevitably slippery here is the necessity of hope in even the gravest of discussions. Kübler-Ross recounts her interviewees' top priorities: "It was the reassurance that everything possible will be done, that they will not be 'dropped,' that there were treatments available, that there was a glimpse of hope—even in the most advanced cases" (49). Hope is, of course, a human need, the meaning of which can transform throughout the dying process in ways crucial to reimagining failure as Halberstam casts it: as a site of new frontiers, creativity, innovation. What is the role of "hope" in the context of a terminal diagnosis? When faced with (nearly) inevitable failure, how does the experience and communication of hope shift and change, and for what purpose?

While there are, again, more conversations on this issue than I can tackle in any comprehensive way, Kübler-Ross gives one particularly poignant example in her famous study. Attempting to describe the critical moment in which a patient stops expressing hope as an indicator of impending death, Kübler-Ross remembers a patient who consistently talked of awaiting "a miracle" (149):

If a patient stops expressing hope, it is usually a sign of imminent death. They may say, "Doctor, I think I have had it," or "I guess this is it," or they may put it like the patient who always believed in a miracle, who one day greeted us with the words, "I think this is the miracle—I am ready now and not even afraid any more." (149)

What Kübler-Ross casts as a concrete "loss of hope" evidenced by the embracing of death—"'I am ready now'"—misses, I think, what is the patient's *recasting* of hope, "'this is the miracle.'" Barbara Ehrenreich's work reminds us of the often-misleading culture of "positive thinking" around breast cancer treatment and diagnosis, and expectations around attitude are often conflated with limited notions of success or failure. Reflecting on Ehrenreich's *Bright-Sided: How the Relentless Promotion of Positive Thinking Has Undermined America*, Halberstam writes,

> Positive thinking is a North American affliction, "a mass delusion" that emerges out of a combination of American exceptionalism and a desire to believe that success happens to good people and failure is just a consequence of a bad attitude rather than structural conditions. (3)

Halberstam finds in the film *Little Miss Sunshine* a powerful, contrary example of the merger of positivity and failure, much in the way Kübler-Ross's patient recasts the awaited miracle. Halberstam describes the unexpected value of protagonist Olive's inevitably failed beauty pageant efforts:

> Olive is destined to fail, and to fail spectacularly. But while her failure could be the source of misery and humiliation, and while it does indeed deliver precisely this, it also leads to a kind of ecstatic exposure of the contradictions of a society obsessed with meaningless competition. (5)

For the patient Kübler-Ross remembers, coming to terms with death is no less miraculous than a spontaneous cure; in fact, it *is* the great, awaited miracle. While I think the contributions of Kübler-Ross's work are incalculable to our cultural education about death and dying, I think easily lost in her insistence that we must face the sad fact of death is space for the "spectacular," for the "ecstatic exposure" of dying as an opportunity for creation, a site of resistance to many of our cultural associations of terminal illness and the dying process with white flag notions of surrender, with giving in and giving up. Exploration of the rhetorics around terminal illness and the collaboration engendered there between Sue and me make room for a consideration of a hopeful, "spectacular" death of another order: in this work—and in other such projects that shake us to our human core—"who" we are and "how" we might behave come productively undone.

Writing and Wishes: Possible Texts

One of the final pieces of writing Sue and I worked on together was her wishes—for her services, for how she wanted objects of affection distributed, for tasks she wanted accomplished—writing work that was inordinately difficult but also poignant for us both. Exactly three weeks before her death, when each day seemed to bring news of another serious medical issue, Sue whispered to me in her hospital room that maybe it'd be a good idea to write some things down: "I've decided something . . ." And I understood immediately, despite her difficulty with asking for much of anything, that this writing-things-down was my province, that this was my role. *Of course I will do this with you.* We had, at this point, spent the last two years in dialogue—both spoken and written—about her illness, weaving our way through ethnographic work that seemed to lead us both along without a map. We found ourselves in her hospital bed, my laptop between us, Sue dictating while I wrote, both of us reading aloud, rephrasing. This was work that took us three hours and that was interrupted by tears and even by laughter at moments of dark absurdity.

This is a scene of writing I will return to again and with fuller attention later in this book, but for the present purpose of thinking about how words might function to reopen or reassign new meaning to failure, I want to reflect on one moment in this last written collaboration. Having just reached a stopping point in the writing process, I was overwhelmed with sadness but also with a kind of awe for Sue's ability to confront her death in such bold, material terms. Her words were at times funny, always confident, and—as was clear by their effect on me as they appeared on my laptop screen—would be a true comfort to those who loved her. I tried to articulate this to her as well as I could: "That you could do this, that you could put words to this, it will bring such comfort to the people who love you most. It says . . . *you've got this.* It's bringing me such comfort right now." She had her arm around me, happy and confident: just as she had become so physically frail by this point, the creation of this text seemed to embolden her and she had become the stronger of the two of us. She squeezed me tighter, looked directly at me, and said, "I know. I won" (Restaino, "Saturday Night").

Sue's recasting of "victory" sends each of us—the one now gone and the other still here writing—into a powerful set of inversions. First, victory is not merely conceptual but also rendered physically in the act of writing, in Sue's ability to create—with my cooperation, as I was not only scribe but also the keeper of the document until after her death—a text that was real, that would be read by others who could affect outcomes that she cared about (for example, her services were as she wanted them; her husband and I split up tasks she wanted completed) and who could be instructed, by her through writing, how *to think* about her death.[5] But more importantly, for purposes of this project, I am interested in the ways in which this writing act embodies, rhetorically, failure as victory, as invention, as a kind of rewriting of terms. My role as both researcher and coauthor of this "final wishes" text serves as a fundamental case in point. In fact, I am—as her scribe and as her keeper of the document—not a rescuer or savior. I had no power to stop her death, nor to protect myself or others who loved her—including her children—from the pain of loss. What, however, my function becomes, I would argue, is rooted in my rhetorical subjectivity, my movement into becoming one who has lost, and who thus comes to write—to continue to produce text, to strive to understand—out of a place or space of loss; this space is uniquely without recognizably traditional answers, victories, or certainties. But it needs writing and sound, too, even if what we are able to perceive is sad or painful. My continued writing and efforts at knowledge making are thus productive in their own right. In a discussion of *Little Miss Sunshine*, Halberstam explains the ultimate value of such "spectacular failure" in the context of Olive's extraordinary loss as a beauty pageant contestant:

> A new kind of optimism is born. Not an optimism that relies on positive thinking as an explanatory engine for social order, nor one that insists upon the bright side at all costs; rather it is a little ray of sunshine that produces shade and light in equal measure and knows that the meaning of one always depends on the meaning of the other. (5)

Part of what is so compelling about Halberstam's explanation here, "the meaning of one always depends on the meaning of the other," is its challenge to expanded method. Such method—for how we do research, how we collaborate with participants, how we write—must take into consideration our shade, as researchers, writers, and people, and the ensuing loose hinges and inevitable failures in the work we produce with the confidence that herein too rests its contribution to what we can learn.

Perhaps even most poignantly, we assign real value to our work by recognizing the ways in which it has the power to overtake us, to confuse us and even to change us professionally and personally. I see an indispensable component of method, then, some daring consideration of the researcher/writer and the scholarly project itself as a shaky, broken by-product of actually doing the work. What this might look like in feminist rhetorical studies must be, I think, work that is informed by a messy engagement with Benjamin's surrender, a willingness to be with others through intersubjective, reflective rhythms. I call also for openness, honesty about the failures that undergird these dances: following a rhythm not only insists that we embrace unpredictability in our work but also comes with the risk of domination. This is at once voluntary and also not voluntary; sometimes we decide we can't or at least *don't want* to continue with our efforts, our line of argument or way of making sense; other times we are simply overcome, with no time to think or decide. We have lost power. Terminal illness is a material enactment of such myriad possibilities for failure that, in the very long shadow it casts, challenges us to seek its unexpected meanings and its light in our living, thinking, writing selves.

Narrative and Resistance

Reading the alternate meaning in a story of terminal illness is hard work in no small part because the emotional pain such illness delivers us easily consumes all else. But it's also hard work because familiar, predictable stories have a seductive and comforting arc. Amid the "pink" war on breast cancer in the United States, the examples of such totalizing narratives are far too numerous to cite in any comprehensive way. Battle metaphors, "sexy" breast cancer, and limited notions of survivorship dominate the popular, national conversation, driven by corporatized powerhouses like Avon's "Walk for the Cure" and the Susan G. Komen Foundation.[6] Still, resistance to these commanding narratives continues to emerge. Reflecting on the loss of a friend, far too young, a disillusioned Erika Anderson writes in the popular culture magazine *Gawker*,

> I will not walk this year. I will not walk next year. I may never walk for breast cancer. For those who do walk, I realize it might not be all about the donations they amass, or about clinging to impossible dreams. . . . That could be good for them. But not for me. And not for dozens who commiserate, for people who are done with the battle metaphor, done with the ferocity of pink, with *the more of us who walk,*

the more of us survive because it is factually inaccurate, a slogan that will not placate us. (3)

Rhodes reminds us again that there's a violence to "narrative inclusion," a move that "seeks to contain difference in order to make it legible, identifiable, and thus acceptable to a normative readership" ("Rhizomes"). Stage IV breast cancer casts its shade on totalizing, easily digestible popular narratives, though often terminal patients are far less visible in the popular media circuit of survivorship and positive thinking promoted by Komen and Avon.

Perhaps even more troublesome, the deaths are nevertheless often recycled into the media engine, not only as honored, remembered names for fund-raising efforts but also in a move that pushes terminal patients into a space of comforting distance for those on the "safe" side of the room. Thus narratives of terminal illness spin predictability and comfort as well: "the more of us who walk" is easily synonymous with "the more of us who are not them." *Those women, over there, the ones who are dying* is a move that isolates difference in ways that, as Rhodes suggests, make it "legible, identifiable, and thus acceptable." We can join the fight against breast cancer in ways that protect us from becoming its victim; we can be "not them" by walking. We can at once understand that terminal patients, the inspirational but ill-fated casualties of the war on breast cancer, exist *over there* while also rooting ourselves firmly in the fight, the walk, the space of "normal" in which they are no longer welcome. Sue was sensitive to this dynamic and, dictating to me her last wishes, refused to occupy this position of iconized fallen warrior. In her words:

> I don't want the word "battle" used at any point during services for me. Nothing like "her courageous fight" or some bullshit. I lived my life the way I wanted to live it in spite of a disease that I had. No heroic stuff . . . NO PINK ANYTHING, ANYWHERE! (Maute, "What I Want")

Rejecting the battle metaphor, Sue also rejected the likely characterization of her own heroism: "no heroic stuff." Embedded here is a hope for privacy, for the claiming of an individualized, *real* life amid a totalizing narrative/disease: "I lived my life . . . in spite . . ." The alternative is a comforting narrative arc, one that makes death not only magical but also "earned" and somehow explainable: though she fought valiantly, the battle was long and she lost "her courageous fight." She is a hero among us, better than us; we can recognize her and also not *be* her. Suddenly we have a story we can live with, one that assures us of our own safety, our welcome inadequacy or lack of heroism, and thus secures our distance from event and players. In rejecting this narrative in my collaboration with Sue, I opened my role as researcher-writer to new vulnerability as well: I became, in my own way and perhaps in terms of my own unique role, unsafe by association.

Exploring the "radical passivity" of masochistic performance art, Halberstam argues for the subversive reclaiming of passivity as a move to control subjectivity, "to actually come undone" (140). In its fullest manifestation, "masochistic fantasy transfers punishments definitively away from the body of the subjugated and onto the body of the oppressor" (144). While Sue's refusal to allow her body, in death, to be marked by pink "*ANYTHING, ANYWHERE!*" or explained through "'her courageous fight' or some bullshit" is clearly a move to disempower "Breast Cancer," in this case Halberstam's "oppressor," her characterization of her death as non-heroic is perhaps most radical. Halberstam explains the ultimate task of the masochistic performance artist in light of "the supposedly irreconcilable tension between pleasure and death": "She refuses to cohere, refuses to fortify herself against the knowledge of death and dying, and seeks instead to be out of time altogether, a body suspended in time, space, desire" (144). Sensitive to how her time might be totalized and explained following her death, Sue moved to redefine it in our last piece of writing together: "It has not been hard. It's only been hard for the past nine months. I have lived a full, fun, crazy life. Nine months is going to dictate the whole rest of the bullshit? No" (Maute, "What I Want"). Here Sue overturns the assumption that her life must have been far more pain than pleasure (destabilizing the long battle narrative that would insist otherwise) and also refuses a kind of colonization of her time, her lifetime, by breast cancer. Though she had breast cancer for over ten years (a sizable portion of anyone's life but especially hers, since it ended in her forties), she rejected her own suffering in that longer period, doling out instead a mere "nine months" as actually "hard." Though suffering and dying *now*, she has not in fact always been; most of her life—including the years with breast cancer—has been "full, fun, crazy," and with this claim she dislocates herself from any reading of time spent, one rendered easily in popular breast cancer narratives and in popular media around the "war on pink" that places her disease and her suffering at the center. She is indeed knowledgeable about her impending death—"I know where I am going. I know what's happening to me"—while she refuses to sanctify this death, to make it in any way tremendous, unusual, or a true, final abuse of her (Maute, "What I Want").

In reclaiming the "time span" of her own suffering, Sue enacts a kind of narrativizing or rescuing of time perhaps reminiscent of Corder's and Newkirk's wishes. However, the tensions that for Halberstam are embedded in radical passivity push us to resee failure for its analytical, activist riches and reorient us to time as ultimately a controlling, limiting force. Essentially, it runs out despite even our best efforts to the contrary. Thus, to what extent is Sue's claiming of time and experience in her last wishes a kind of radical acquiescence of sorts, passive in ways that avoid participation in the stories that bring us easy comfort, particularly since these very stories would cast her as a hero? Conversely, how might Sue's resistance to her own heroism function as a Benjaminian surrender, one that is "precisely not *to* the object or other," in this case breast cancer ("From Many into One" 189)? In "From Many into One," Benjamin explores her own writing process in light of the experience of surrender, which she describes as "this paradoxical relation of losing and finding the self . . . wherein liberation comes through acceptance" (189). Benjamin rectifies this paradox by surrendering to a writing process clearly inspired by Whitman: "To integrate differently my different selves, to contain my multitudes" (196). What is most striking about Benjamin's claim is the potential for the containment of contradiction, that in fact contradiction—at once losing and finding—might be *the* thing, the source of greatest meaning, a way of breaking the narratives, and the very roles, that might otherwise erase us (*she was a hero among us; the writer-researcher as rescuer*).

Benjamin goes on in "From Many into One" to use the metaphor of Bach's tendency in musical composition to explore dissonance even though "no matter how far out he swings, he will always return to his theme" (199). It is the distance, in fact, between dissonance and harmony—for Benjamin, the space we must traverse—that stands to teach us most fully:

> For me, what is interesting in writing, finally, like composing, is taking a theme that involves contradiction and raising it to a higher level, in order to experience this stretch, this tension. The point is to see how much dissonance you can create and still resolve the harmony, because the greater the dissonance the more intense the resolution. (199)

For my part in this book, I suppose I am willing to press on—perhaps even break—the hope for any "resolution" whatsoever, though I am also of course compelled to embrace the narrative Sue herself rewrote/ reclaimed in the spirit of dissonance, should that be considered her own subversive resolution of sorts. Still, the challenge posed here to feminist research methodology is rich, and in resisting the narratives that bring us the most comfort, we are able to ask a series of key questions: What if there is no way to explain suffering over time? In other words, what if the time spent (however long or short) fails to produce more clarity, some kind of understanding, legitimizing, or acceptance of the pain (or *any* data, for that matter)? To what extent is resistance to a smooth, meaning-making narrative, one about heroism or bravery, also a resistance to suffering as "legible, reliable, and thus acceptable"? What knowledge making (perhaps we can call this "resolution") is possible on the far edge of dissonance? What are the possibilities for what we can learn when the notes become unexpected, unanticipated, grating even—truly dissonant? *Who* are we—as writers, as researchers—when we lose ourselves, our research agendas, even our collaborators, and why does this "who" matter as we think about the work of knowledge making?

Disorderly Methods and Broken Genres

I am reminded here of Eileen Schell's introduction to *Rhetorica in Motion*, where she describes "feminist rhetorical methods and methodologies as movement, as motion, and as action," which, for Patricia Bizzell, require "'methods which violate some of the most cherished conventions of academic research, most particularly in bringing the person of the research, her body, her emotions, and dare one say, her soul into the work'" (qtd. in Schell and Rawson 4–6). While these moves call for a kind of nontraditional methodology, outside of what we might consider appropriate or established practice, ultimately my paradoxical goal in this book is to standardize or at least welcome methodological "violation" of, as Bizzell notes, our "cherished conventions." The risks here are myriad: for example, Corder gets tangled when he "rewrites" method via Grandma Corder, whose process of quilt making happened "without the aid of authors who want to be sure that the world gets corrected . . . to be sure we define the quiltmaker's art in their way" ("I in Mine" 259). Ultimately Corder assigns his grandmother the authority of methodological invention; it's a fine line, though, between bucking and also re-creating the system. Corder knows as much—"I know that in trying to hold things, I too will vanish" (260)—and so the challenge becomes expanding the possibilities for method without merely overturning it and re-creating hierarchical systems.[7]

While I will spend more time on the issue of methodological splits in my field of rhetoric-composition in the following chapter, the blurring of methodological practice more broadly opens possibility for an equally shifting, multiple researcher-writer subject as well. I offer my own subjectivity up as one model for this hybridization as a research and writing practice, as well as a way of embodying my identity on these pages. I work here with qualitative methods for data gathering, like interview and transcription, to create what are essentially primary source materials that I then read like a humanities scholar. Along this vein, and while even social scientists may not always work with a coding scheme, I feel it is worth noting that I did not code the many pages of transcribed conversations between Sue and me. I have instead worked closely with these texts as any humanities scholar might, in hopes of studying a kind of nuance, appropriate for a small-scale study of this sort, that I believe is most fully accessed by close reading and textual analysis. I am thus working, in a sense, "out of order"—at least as order might be construed by *either* the humanities or the social sciences. In either case, I am violating some piece of standard practice in order to create something entirely other but also distinctly hybridized.

Queer praxes for writing and research offer a useful frame for building what I am calling here "disorderly methods and broken genres," and in fact I might argue that queer praxes affirm for us the very necessity of building such subversions into our work. I want to stress that my move here is not to propose a method, per se: there are research designs surely most suited to traditional social scientific methods, for example, and those methods continue to serve our field well as we seek certain kinds of knowledge. Rather, my goal—across methods—is to insist on increased focus on the researcher role in itself. My argument is thus that when we constrain ourselves methodologically we are also likely to constrain ourselves subjectively.[8] Halberstam quotes an interview with the performance artist Nao Bustamante, "'The work that I do is about not knowing the equipment, and not knowing that particular balance, and then finding it as I go'" (143). This serves as a working, practical description of Stuart Hall's "low theory," which Halberstam claims as a distinctly queer frame: "It makes peace with the possibility that alternatives dwell in the murky waters of a counterintuitive, often impossibly dark and negative realm of critique and refusal" (2). The *how* and *what* in my collaboration with Sue and in my work in this book continuously affirm this frame. The topic itself, terminal illness, is taboo. My writing style is a combination of narrative chunks, broken up with qualitative data, broken up with scholarly citation, and—all of it, really—is laced with real emotion. The boundaries between researcher and participant are very much destabilized, embodying in fact some of Kirsch's warnings ("close friends do not usually arrive with a tape-recorder" [Cotterill qtd. in Kirsch 2166]). Our relationship was one of real intimacy and connection: I loved Sue deeply (still do); she was my friend; I was by her side in her last hours. These notions of "who" thread substantively through "what"—the methods employed—and shape meaning in ways unique to a collaboration founded on intimacy and subjective transformation. In fact I could argue that there were multiple transformations for each of us in the course of our partnership. Still the central change-over-time was, for Sue, movement toward and through dying and for me movement toward and through loss; these movements had to happen rhetorically and materially in concert with the other.

Such unique motion demands unique methods, which of course yield ways of reading and writing that echo the energy of the work itself. Running alongside my research and writing *in and for* this book have been (continue to be) a series of informal texts. The first group of texts is my own reflective writing on my experiences with Sue both during her illness and after her death. About two weeks after her passing I started a document titled "What It Feels Like," and the content is exactly as the title suggests: grief, longing, confusion as embodied, day-to-day, shifting experience; as of this writing I continue to update this log. Also deeply important is my long-term correspondence with Lisa Ede, an expert on feminist rhetorics and praxes, who has been a constant mentor to me for the last several years and an indispensable source of wisdom and care through my experience with Sue. In her own scholarly work, Ede's long-standing collaboration with Andrea Lunsford—of which the latter writes in a letter to Ede, "I can no more think of giving up our writerly ways than I could of giving up breathing . . . or eating"—sets a precedent for feminist collaboration in text as a source of knowledge making and also mutual sustenance (Lunsford and Ede 66).[9] In their essay "Border Crossings: Intersections of Rhetoric and Feminism," coauthored with Cheryl Glenn, they insist that "feminist theory has consistently challenged any public/private distinction, arguing that knowledge based in the personal, in lived experience, be valued and accepted as important and significant" (Ede et al. 286). In fact the running email threads between Lisa and me fully enact this claim, lacing scholarly discussions with reports from the realities of each of our lives, details sometimes trivial and at other times deeply meaningful.

Our written conversation these last years, at once emotional and intellectual, has been a rich space in which this book has taken root and through which, certainly most importantly, I have grown as a reader, writer, and person. It was Lisa who pointed me to Jessica Benjamin's work, who fielded my first questions about the arc of scholarly attention to the personal in rhetoric-composition, and who has continued to affirm for me that this project—with its particular blend of intimacy and research—has a place in discourses about feminist methods in rhetorical studies. I suppose I think of the scholarly role Lisa has occupied in my process as akin to Eli Goldblatt's claims about authority in developing writers in *'Round My Way*: "Authors must always fulfill two roles: they act both as *representers* of a socially shared and institutionalized reality and also as *representatives* of sponsoring institutions" (25). My work in this book relies on a destabilization of "institution," taking terminal illness itself as an institution of sorts, one laden with cultural and social assumptions, while also working across different though more traditional institutions: hospital, home, chemo clinic, hospice center, and university. Perhaps most resonant with this idea of "sponsorship" is the fact that I have been able to go forward in this work—my own role betwixt and between, as Goldblatt describes—in no small part *because* Lisa has validated it; she is senior to me professionally, a woman I admire and respect intellectually and personally. That I might be able to give some integrated scholarly voice to these myriad and at times competing institutions owes a debt to Lisa's authorization of this work for me, via our written dialogue, as legitimate within feminist rhetorical studies. These dynamics are not trivial but rather inform and shape the meaning and power of our dialogue, its influence and value for me.

Most profound and, I want to argue, inseparable from the intellectual conversation between us has been the space our written dialogue has made for the emotional experience of loss. My writing to Lisa has functioned as the place where I gave some shape, in words, to the pain Sue endured, to my own experience of helplessness, and ultimately to the terrible silence that followed Sue's death. I detailed to Lisa the story of writing down Sue's wishes in the hospital, which was one of the most anguishing and yet also loving experiences of my life; I wrote her with anxious updates as one setback seemed to follow another; and ultimately I wrote her as I was leaving the hospice center following Sue's death. This last example was my shortest piece of writing to Lisa ever: "This morning I lost my great friend. Finding my way home from hospice" (Restaino, "Re: She's gone"). As consuming and disorienting as Sue's absence was in those first moments, Lisa had worked to prepare me. Just four weeks before Sue's death Lisa wrote, "You will know what to do.

You can't anticipate how you will feel, or how Sue will feel leaving this world, or how her family will feel, or how others will feel. But you will know what to do" (Ede, "Re: The latest"). And in fact she was right, or at least she has been right to the extent that "what to do" has been akin for me to Bustamante's description of her artistic method, "'not knowing that particular balance, and then finding it as I go'" (qtd. in Halberstam 143). I read Bustamante's words here as a method both for grief *and* for research and writing along the fault lines of illness, intimacy, and loss. Ultimately if we embrace Bustamante's "finding it as we go," we become new agents and new researchers, over and over again for as long as we move through the work.

In no small part this "finding it as I go" has taken place via my written correspondence with Lisa, which spans more email threads than I could bother to count. In what ways does this "external" (to the formal scholarly text), nontraditional, conversational writing depend upon surrender as Benjamin describes it? To what extent might it be the essential repository for my many methodological failures, for my struggles at understanding, for the many attempts I have required to think and rephrase in order to move forward both intellectually and personally? Anne Ruggles Gere borrowed the term "extracurriculum" to describe writing "beyond the academy," which she claims is "constructed by desire, by the aspirations and imaginations of its participants" and capable of "transformations in personal relationships" (80). The ever-growing body of research on community-based writing has done much to further Gere's foundational call that we embrace composition's extracurriculum as an essential piece of writing development. As an indispensable element of my own disorderly method, I expose and point at the extracurriculum of this book, which includes an unruly, grief-filled, and searching epistolary text in which I have been able to share something like Benjamin's "third" where "what just happened" can be explored, questioned, given words that at times have exceeded what Sue and I could do merely together, so consumed were we by the real-time progression of her illness and her approaching death.[10] Furthermore, my correspondence with Lisa also has sustained a dialogic mental space that has buoyed and supported me in Sue's real absence; it has outlived her in real time. This is at once a model of Benjamin's third, a space that has required of me—and of Lisa, too, I think—a kind of surrender, a following of threads and rhythms, while it has also expanded our circle to include what I'd describe as a triangulated dialogue: Sue/me and me/Lisa. As this writing has found its way into this book, and as its content, idea generation, and exploratory style have and will continue to shape my own writing here and now—are in fact shaping and making *me*—I see this correspondence to be an inseparable, nontraditional genre that is part of this overall work.

Never Whole: Shattered and Multiple Identities

To reclaim the position of witness and restore the lawful third ultimately requires a tension between "I could never imagine doing such a thing" and "I could imagine doing it." Accepting badness is part of the journey for those who actually expose themselves to civil rights violations, collective trauma, and indeed horrors with the hope of witnessing or actually helping. (Benjamin, "Discarded and the Dignified" 3)

Jessica Benjamin's current work engages in repair of collective trauma and includes activist efforts focused particularly on opening dialogue between Palestinians and Israelis in the war-torn Middle East. Her recent essay, the six-part installation "The Discarded and the Dignified," explores this work and its theoretical underpinnings.[11] Inseparable from the healing work of conversation around trauma and violence are Benjamin's concepts of intersubjectivity, the moral third, and a breakdown of complementary dynamics between perpetrators and victims. As Benjamin describes above, there is a conceptual leap needed for the healing of collective trauma that requires a breach, a bridging, of "badness": in fact the lines must blur in exploring the dark recesses of the other's mind, pain, and capacity for harm. Building on Benjamin's current work, I want to argue here that any effort to understand how rhetoric functions inside terminal illness also requires a blurring of boundaries, most crucially our respective identities as "healthy" or "ill." In many ways, like the seeming inconceivability of Benjamin's "I could never imagine," we must find ways to step as far over the dividing lines between us—though we can't live another's disease—to destabilize the fantasy of the impermeable, indestructible body. This requires not only a shifting subjectivity but the coexistence of multiple subjectivities, one that fractures any singular body as fully whole, controllable, or totally knowable.

Sue often felt the impulse to comfort me as I witnessed the devastations that terminal breast cancer wreaked on her body. She'd lean forward after a particularly hard conversation or in the aftermath of some awful medical episode or intervention, and she'd whisper: "Don't worry. I'm our statistic" (as I write that I realize I can't even date it via my interview transcripts because it was something she said with casual frequency). This pained me, desperate as I was for her not to be *any* statistic, ours or otherwise; yet it also wrapped me in a strange, shameful comfort. Trained as a mathematician, Sue could often craft her support and her assurances in scientific, quantifiable terms; there was comfort to be found in numbers. Her own numbers, her statistical "chances," seemed to get smaller and further away, of course, over time; it was no wonder, given her deep reserves, that she took the opportunity presented by that shrinking gap to point out just how comparatively *big* the numbers were for those she loved. However, when reflecting on herself, her own situation, her language shifted in ways that cast my mathematical comfort into a tailspin. "It was never," she said in one of our earlier interviews, "'Why me?' but 'Why not me?' Disease and tragedy are non-discriminatory" (Maute, personal interview, 31 May 2013). In his "On Cancer and Freshman Composition," Corder maintains that, in recognizing shared ground—"we all already have cancer"—we have the power to prevent at least a metaphorical cancer from unruly growth by allowing for disagreement and difference, all the while keeping our distinct selves intact (6). Corder insists that "identity is always to be saved . . . cherished" (8). My work with Sue in the context of terminal illness convinces me that Corder in fact is fruitlessly and perhaps even dangerously hopeful here and that his separatist construct negates the generative, rhetorical capacity for chaos and surrender. Communicative intimacy amid terminal illness demands that both bodies be destabilized: what has happened to you could happen to me, or, in parallel to Benjamin's work in collective trauma, "I could never imagine doing such a thing/I could imagine . . ." In this material destabilization, we reach new conceptual ground.

Even in the case of Benjamin's work on collective trauma, the canvas for understanding and exchange happens amid and between material bodies. In both violence and terminal illness, it is the body that functions as the site of the infraction, the observable, suffered damage. The body invites intimacy and vulnerability in ways that are essential to destabilizing what, for Benjamin, are our otherwise "us/them" complementary relations. In "The Discarded and the Dignified," Benjamin recounts a documentary film, *One Day after Peace*, that explores the story of a grieving mother's quest to forgive the man who killed her daughter in a random militia attack amid South African apartheid violence. When the mother is finally invited to the soldier's village, an act of deep reconciliation, his sister expresses disappointment upon learning that the woman brought with her a sleeping bag so as not to burden her with the work of cleaning sheets: "'I did not intend to wash the sheets. I wanted to sleep in the sweat of the woman who forgave my brother'" (9). For Benjamin, it is the "visceral metaphor of skin and sweat" that "explif[ies] the overcoming of bodily separation on which we found our dissociation from the other's pain" (9). When we "move to overcome" such separation—for example when we refuse to separate out terminal breast cancer patients from "survivors" or from those "who walk"—we inevitably blur binary identity lines and open ourselves more fully to understanding the other. Benjamin explains, "The move from dissociated to embodied language and affect creates a third in which the binary of perpetrator and victim, invulnerable and vulnerable breaks down, as the suffering body itself is dignified through acceptance of pain" (2).

In the case of terminal illness, for Sue and me this meant the breaking down of dichotomies like healthy versus ill, university versus hospital, "whole" versus augmented body, and researcher versus participant. Each of these is ultimately rooted in issues of identity. I return here again to the scene of a terrible internal bleed and its aftermath, a blood transfusion: we sat together in her hospital room, both of us scared and exhausted. I offered her a few words about how tough she had been, how exemplary through it all. She looked at me with a lot of conviction and said, "You would do it the same way, Jess" (Restaino, "Reflection: Week of 7/7/14"). Her words settled on me as much a gift as a burden. *Would I?*, I thought. *Am I*, I wondered, *strong like her—can she see something I can't?* But soon, my internal questions turned more fearfully to *Must I?* That Sue saw in me—whether right or wrong—a capacity for endurance, for strength amid great suffering, also marked me: just as I might be strong like her, I could be vulnerable, sick, like her too. With this move, she brought me to her side, destabilizing the "hero" narrative and its tendency to separate the hero figure from those who are weaker, the fearful "survivors" huddled together in amazement at the fallen hero and her great battle, the one they never could have fought so valiantly. In resisting my assertions of her own exceptionalism, Sue insisted that I experience my own potentiality for both great strength and great suffering. And this was, and remains, a source of mixed pride and fear for me, an experience of "unknowing" myself, as Rhodes and Alexander might call it. But it has also been absolutely essential to our connection, stretching the limits of our rhetorical understanding and intimacy. Such unknowing rewrites my role: when I work with our artifacts, when I write, I am open to what Charon calls "porous transit" (220).[12]

The willingness to move from "having" to loss, from certainty to uncertainty—*transit*, to draw again on Charon—comes with necessary acceptance of great vulnerability. Halberstam describes Yoko Ono's work of performance art *Cut Piece* as a "commitment to the fragment of the whole over any fantasy of future wholeness" (138). Halberstam goes on to detail the piece in which Ono invites audience members, one at a time, to cut away pieces of her clothing while she sits still, allowing the fragmentation of her garments and thus her increasing nakedness. Halberstam cites these "cutting gestures" as an "antisocial feminism" that "dedicates itself completely and ferociously to the destruction of self and other" (138). Sue's refusal of her own exceptionalism, her insistence that I would "do it the same way," functions similarly as a kind of loving destruction of each of us. In fact we could not understand each other as fully as we did—all differences considered—if I could not do more than witness her suffering as entirely outside of my own body's capabilities. By bringing me more closely into her own intimate circle of pain, Sue destroyed my comforting self-identification as unreachable, impervious to the sort of illness and suffering she endured. I was no longer on the winning side of statistics; I was now—and I remain—with her in the space of *why not me* or, as Benjamin casts it, coexistent with *I could never imagine/I could imagine*. Ultimately the destabilization of identity, the fracturing of identity, and our subsequent containment of multiple selves (at once healthy/ill, researcher/participant) must function as indelible components of method in work that seeks to explore the rhetorical intimacies and dark corners, the topics, like terminal illness, that resist being fully "knowable." In my work here I am, simply, possible: I write and learn from this unsure place.

From Here to There: Surrendering into Method

While much remains unexplored about how we might enact a methodology for surrender and failure, as well as how we might work from a place of our own fractured, multiple selves, my hope is that the concepts here as well as my lived experiences with Sue serve as a frame in which others can explore their own models. Still, in the remaining chapters my goals will be threefold: to situate the need for and potential riches of deeper conversations about the researcher-writer self, particularly as we surrender into hybridized methods given those projects that demand of us real intimacy and risk; to more fully flesh out what this transformation and resulting knowledge look like in my work with Sue; and to examine the limits and possibilities for how we might extend such investigations forward. I am, as a scholar, a writer, and a learner, myself notably wary of moves to establish generalized knowledge, which I tend to see as boundary lines designed to demarcate "discipline" in ways that undermine the roots of my own discipline, rhetoric-composition, as inherently hybridized, interdisciplinary work.[13] My impulse, instead, is to in fact claim our mobility, our essential capacity for seepage and spilling over, capacities that I think mark work in the field of rhetoric-composition as a disciplinary "identity" of sorts.[14] On the radical (or perhaps, I might suggest, not so radical) end of this spectrum is our human capacity for love and care in our work. This challenge is thus about making room for human possibility, need, and agency without mandating a practice or set of ideological systems around method that ultimately become limits, lines drawn rather than gates flung open.

Such "making room" comes easier to certain kinds of research work over others. Feminist discussions of method, for example, have long explored nontraditional approaches to ethnography perhaps given the more inviting, more flexible emphasis on narrative inherent in this work. Patricia Sullivan reminds us of the rich "unreliability" of ethnography in her essay "Ethnography and the Problem of the 'Other'" with the questions "Who is telling the story, the researcher or the researched? After all, whose story is it to tell?" (104). While I will spend more focused time on these methodological divides in the following chapter, I hope it is clear in this book so far that I have no confident answer to Sullivan's questions. I know that Sue's "breast cancer story" is not mine to tell in any succinct, orderly way. I also find myself consistently slipping in and out of the role of researcher, often losing and then excavating versions of my approach, my understandings, my relationship to knowledge-making in ways that surely make me at times the "subject" of this book; one of my key goals throughout this book is thus to lay bare this subject, my rendered self on these pages, amid my own porous transit(s). At other times, of course, my role functions more predictably as I transcribe interviews, synthesize data with existent scholarship in the field, and attempt to situate this project as legitimate scholarly work in rhetoric-composition. Even as I do this, however, admittedly I find myself unable to stay put, moving in and out of cultural studies, feminist psychoanalytical theory, queer theory, and etymology. Accordingly, I hope my many moves here might signal an invitation to scholars outside of rhetoric-composition *into* this interdisciplinary, diversely informed field.

Perhaps my scholarly unreliability, in a sense, has its deepest roots in grief itself, which I see as intimately bound up in this work. Real, sustained grief indeed engages us alternatingly across Benjamin's concepts: surrender and submission, at once shuttling us along rhythmically, discovering over and again the depth of our loss, while periodically dominating us, stilling and silencing us with the incomprehensibility of absence. We are at once actors and acted upon, as researchers and writers, when we pursue what Halberstam calls the "more chaotic realm of knowing and unknowing," that rich, epistemological space from which we might work through "shade and light in equal measure." In *Precarious Life*, Judith Butler captures I think quite succinctly the ways in which we move into, and then are inevitably moved by, grief and longing: "I tell a story about the relations I choose, only to expose, somewhere along the way, the way I am gripped and undone by these very relations. My narrative falters, as it must" (23). Indeed real grief is ultimately unresolvable. I see such inherently human experience at the heart of any feminist work to explore rhetoric at its most intimate. My project in this book is thus not merely to offer methodological possibilities for our faulty efforts at knowledge making but to explore the roots of those efforts in our own agency, as doers of research and writers of texts, as those upended and thus rendered by work that undoes us.

BLOODWORK
(A TEXT MESSAGE)

Very interesting morning . . . I'm doing well. Interesting in a profound way. As heinous as my life looks on the outside, I love my life . . . and these feelings are without being . . . morphine induced!!! (Maute, "Re: Interesting morning")

STAGE II

BUILDING AND BREAKING

METHODOLOGICAL CONTRADICTIONS
AND UNANSWERABLE QUESTIONS

> GLENN: I was really aware of ending with a quotation because that is another thing I have learned somewhere along the line. You never end with a quotation. You always end with your own words. Your interpretation of a quotation is all right, but you never end with a quotation.
>
> RESEARCHER: Then why did you end with a quotation?
>
> GLENN: Because it worked. It just worked there.
> —*Mike Rose, Writer's Block: The Cognitive Dimension*

The original *Writer's Block: The Cognitive Dimension*, a twice-published cognitive study of writer's block, was first published in 1984, a revised version of Rose's dissertation and an effort to "think carefully and closely about the process of getting words onto paper" (xvi). In the 2009 reissue of the study, Rose offers an insightful prologue in which he explores his initial motivations behind the work, how he might do the study differently today, and his hopes for research in rhetoric-composition going forward. Most crucial, perhaps, is Rose's use of a cognitive perspective that, he notes, has faced criticism for its "attempts to rationalize human behavior and . . . subject it to technical control" and thus "exclude it from analysis of history and social context" (xx). The deeper tension in Rose's study, and thus its particular value for my purposes here, takes root in his call in the prologue for a "hybridization" of research methods and the need to at times destabilize "rule or plan" (xxi). Rose's discussion of order and procedure as they appear (or fail to appear) in the experience of writer's block, and as they function in his very technical study, becomes, in his prologue to the reissue, a way of also talking about research methodology. In Rose's captivating "low blocker," Glenn, we see quite poignantly the rehearsed familiarity with acquired rules—"You never end with a quotation"—and the bucking of those very rules on grounds that are seemingly intuitive, almost guttural: "It just worked" (63).

I am intrigued by such conviction, what I see as the undermining of well-known expectations and rules on a premise that is—to draw on Sondra Perl's term—"felt sense," essentially a feeling, and one not easily quantifiable or even replicable from one study to the next. Rose's call in his prologue for "hybrid methodologies" acknowledges the presence of "seemingly unabridgeable philosophical differences" across certain disciplinary approaches; however, as he notes, "that tension itself would be worthy of exploration from the inside" (xv). I want to argue in this chapter that an essential component of such exploration "from the inside" and an ensuing form of hybrid method might include an intangible or "felt sense," at times the confounding quality of the work, one born through collaboration between researcher and participant, between writer and page, in ways that make space for the slippery, fractured drive *to do* the work. Our intuitive movement through these broken praxes might be in fact epistemological: we are coming to know a series of relational "whos"—researcher/writer/participant—via the transitional processes of searching and knowing.

In this chapter I have four central goals, all of which I hope will prove mere openings designed to invite others' continued discussion and exploration of cross-disciplinary research approaches and experience. The first is to examine this phenomenon of "methodological release," first as it occurs in Rose's research participant, Glenn, and next as a potential metaphor for doing or orienting to our work more broadly. My sense is that our tendency *not* to build into our research and writing processes a personal "release" button of sorts, exemplified by Glenn's gut sense, can cut off possibilities for how we might evolve as researcher-writers, particularly when we approach our work with clear-cut rules and expectations. As a second goal, then, I will explore the potential limits and losses of more scripted approaches while resisting, as Rose does, "wholesale dismissal" of *any* method (xiv). In fact, for Rose, our field "invites a vibrant interdisciplinarity," and thus "the kinds of issues we study in rhetoric and composition are so complex that no single method or perspective . . . can illuminate all we need to know" (xiv). My deeper hope here is that in exposing the mixed nature of my own work, I might also invite others who write and research outside of my field to find something here in rhetoric-composition that resonates with their own interdisciplinary standpoints.

My third step is most crucial to this book, which is to argue that when we release our processes as need dictates, we stand to enter into epistemological work that is about what we can't necessarily explain or fully "know," just as Glenn is essentially confounded (and even contradictory) in his discussion of how and why he chooses to end his essay as he does. This movement, more importantly, into that which exasperates us—rhetorically, intellectually, and perhaps also emotionally—is urgently deserving of our scholarly attention. Such a scholarly precipice occasions its own methodology, an open process through which researchers can more fully investigate their own experiences: the confusions, the cracks, the falling-to-pieces of the work itself that indeed not only function as knowledge making in feminist rhetorical study but also remake the researcher-writer with newly defined roles, responsibilities, and capacities for doing the work itself. Periodically in this discussion I will weave analytically and narratively through my relationship with Sue as we tried to move together through her experience of terminal illness in writing and in talk. As Sue's illness progressed, I struggled extensively with the helplessness of my role as witness. However, in this role as witness I was led along by Sue's versatility, her movement through and within the increasing physical limits of her body. Such movement functions as a model for me as researcher-writer on the edge of comprehension and also as a person confronting loss. I will pay closer attention to this phenomenon later in this chapter. While I believe discussions of feminist research methodologies have long established the groundwork for reflexivity in our work, as a fourth goal I argue that the continuous evolution of a "who"—a set of roles we might occupy in any given research collaboration—is intimately bound up in our willingness to work along these epistemological edges.[1]

Methodological Release: Surrender and the Irrational

While Glenn is a conventionally successful school-based writer—"'look at those papers I wrote in high school—all those As'"—he is quite unreliable when it comes to explaining what he does (and why he does it) on the page (Rose, *Writer's Block* 63). This unreliability is his great contribution to a discussion of methodology and expected outcomes. Noting that Glenn has an "ideal essay pattern" in mind, Rose nevertheless applauds his ability to "modif[y] or abandon these characteristics

. . . as his barriers and discoveries demands" (66). But perhaps most rich are Glenn's conflicted attempts at explaining his method and his relationship to his work. At times he describes his commitment to his writing and to the decisions he makes as a writer as "not that important to me" and notes that he could "write on something that I did not really feel strongly about" (68, 63). Still, his faith in his writing, the confidence he has in the process itself, is significant: "I just really want to get the ideas out and just go, go, go with that, and something good will come out of it" (61). Rose pursues Glenn's motivations and his conflicted relationship with his written products in ways that, I would argue, further illuminate the intimate, connected, and yet contradictory relationship Glenn has with his writing:

> This does not mean to say that Glenn will write anything with equal abandon; as was seen, he felt better about a new, more accurate, fourth paragraph than about a falsely optimistic original. Asked about the motive for this revision, he replied, "I am interested in my own mind." Still, "I am really just lazy, most of the time, in my writing. I go a lot for what will sound good and sometimes it works. Usually it works." (68)

In Glenn's search for explanations for his choice methods, there's a mix of dismissal, investment, and, perhaps above all, a gut sense or faith. Not only will "something good . . . come out of it" if Glenn just "goes" with his writing, but he describes a gut or intuitive sense: "what will sound good." We can't be quite sure what this means, whether writing that "sounds good" is merely a collection of impressive vocabulary words or something far more substantive, though the assessment of Glenn's writing by both teachers and Rose himself suggests the latter. Most significant, I'd argue, is Glenn's assertion "I am interested in my own mind" as an overarching motivation for his revision efforts. While aware of a rule-bound frame, Glenn demonstrates—and Rose celebrates—an ability to "modify or abandon" these rules on grounds that are often more easily felt than explained and, yet, a vehicle for the pursuit of "my own mind." Perhaps the "laziness" Glenn describes is rooted more in the difficulty he might feel in trying to explain such an intangible rationale of sorts, one grounded essentially in his own process of becoming "me" in this text, at this moment, and under these relational circumstances.

While I admit I wonder whether all our methodological processes have an element of this intangibility, I am well aware this is not a claim I am able to make. I would like to insist, instead, that we learn to recognize those research and writing experiences that call for attunement and responsiveness to that which dismantles our inherited, respected toolboxes and even our seemingly defined roles. In their discussion of feminist interviewing practices, Marjorie DeVault and Glenda Gross explain that this methodological dismantling can have its roots in the openness and vulnerability of the researcher to human experience.

> Active listening means more than just physically hearing or reading; rather, it is a fully engaged practice that involves not only taking in information via speech, written words, or signs, but also actively processing it—allowing that information to affect you, baffle you, haunt you, make you uncomfortable, and take you on unexpected detours, "away from abstract . . . bloodless, professionalized questions," toward peoples, knowledge, and experiences that have been disavowed, overlooked, and forgotten. (182)

My collaboration with Sue exemplifies such dismantling well. In fact, my initial trepidation toward the work, my uncertainty about the usefulness of my questions or the potential contribution such engagement might stand to make in Sue's life, signals much of my divergence from where the responsible qualitative researcher might begin. And certainly as our collaboration and relationship deepened alongside Sue's illness, so too did my own sense of confusion and impending loss. As I wrote in correspondence with Lisa Ede:

> Sometimes I don't know whether her push to live, for real, breaks my heart or fills it. I think it's both. But if I pay attention to her and not to my own feelings, I know what her message is and how she wants it understood. (Restaino, "Re: Small Update")

Of course, such refocusing away from myself—*if I pay attention to her and not to my own feelings*—seems a potential resistance on my part to do just what DeVault and Gross advise: "[Allow] that information to affect you, baffle you, haunt you, make you uncomfortable, and take you on unexpected detours." The sicker Sue became, the more such resistances on my part failed to work. My struggle in that early July email to Lisa would be one of my last stands against my own bafflement and discomfort. The remaining weeks of Sue's life would bring her physical suffering that I could not understand. These weeks would also deliver her to a place of resolve, a kind of clarity of focus at the end of her life that would increasingly generate a role reversal between us. As she approached her own death and as I approached what would be the loss of one of the most meaningful relationships of my life, she would ultimately comfort me.

The complex dynamics—rhetorical, material, emotional—that would drive this progression in our relationship exceed the bounds of what we think of as traditional approaches to research. In other words, "information"—to draw on DeVault and Gross's language—became increasingly unrecognizable or at least misaligned to where our collaboration began. I want to emphasize that this misalignment was generative and offers a more expansive notion of both research and the roles we occupy along the way. For the sake of contrast, I would like to return to Peter Smagorinsky's 2008 essay, "The Method Section as Conceptual Epicenter in Constructing Social Science Research Reports," in which, again, Smagorinsky insists that "studies work best when an author poses a limited set of answerable questions and then designs the paper around them" (405). In every way, my collaboration with Sue was a project that failed to anticipate the answers to its own questions, one that in fact lost control of the questions, which seemed instead to tumble out between us. Our timing, too, was from the "start" out of joint: Sue and I began our formal, recorded interview process months after we began our collaboration. Before we sat down for our first interview, she had visited a class of mine and written a revealing, reflective piece for my undergraduates about her relationship to her body and her athleticism, and we had a rolling dialogue about her illness and all the connections that kept unfolding following that first class visit. That it took Sue and me until the spring that followed my summer class to actually sit together in my office for our first recorded "interview," despite our months of rich conversation, speaks to the likely absence of the linearity Smagorinsky describes. I have retraced the opening of this first recorded conversation, listening and reading again, and it begins with my asking Sue to reread the piece she originally wrote for my students months before. I then prompt her, "So you just read that . . . how would you add to or revise it now?" (Maute, personal interview, 31 May 2013). Given that this piece of writing was, originally, a response to the questions posed on my course syllabus, my thought was that this could be a fine starting place for extending and building upon those initial framing questions.

Sue's response, however, quickly pushed us beyond the confines of that preliminary frame. She begins by stating, "Well, I wouldn't go back and change anything, but I would add more to where this ended about where I am today" (Maute, personal interview, 31 May 2013). "Today," Sue explains, involves an added "spiritual and emotional piece," which perhaps was always there but which her illness has brought into a "culmination." Again, hanging to my focusing questions—though clearly off any kind of script—I ask: "So, does this more spiritual component impact your relationship with your body? Where do you locate yourself in your body?" My goal here was of course to be responsive to what Sue had to say while working to pull us toward the initial framing questions that motivated my course and Sue's first piece of writing. This move is not unprecedented, and in her major work on feminist methodology, *Liberating Method*, DeVault advocates for "involvement" as an "element of method" in the interview process that, ultimately, might deliver feminist scholarship toward a "more disciplined use of the personal" (71).

Already, then, in Sue's responses and even in my questions during our first recorded interview, I felt the pull away from solid ground and Smagorinsky's urging that we pursue "answerable questions." On the heels of my questions about her relationship to her body and her "location" in it, Sue answers:

> From early on, I didn't get angry at God. It was never "Why me?" but "Why not me?" Disease and tragedy are non-discriminatory. I'm not angry at God. I do believe in free will. It may not exactly be what was supposed to happen. . . . I feel like I'm learning how thoughts affect the body, down to the cellular level. Thoughts get changed into chemicals, hormones, throughout your body . . . so that's a daily struggle. There's always a kneejerk reaction, but when I'm able to step outside of that . . . I can step out and analyze. (Maute, personal interview, 31 May 2013)

Here Sue operates between the conceptual and material, working to articulate a relationship that might give me some sense of her "location" somewhere in the middle, or somehow composed of both the abstract and the concrete. Most compelling here is the movement in Sue's words from the completely spiritual—"not angry at God"—to the scientific— "how thoughts affect the body, down to the cellular level." What results is a blend of the spiritually inexplicable, chance ("disease and tragedy are non-discriminatory"), and the quantifiable, chemicals and hormones. There's a mental struggle always underway, that "kneejerk reaction," but if able to fight off a purely emotional response, Sue is able to "step out and analyze." Such analysis, however, can involve any, and maybe all, of the realms she inhabits: God's role in her disease; chaos and chance, mere bad luck; or the relationship between her thinking process (negative or positive) and its potential impact on her material body.

I occupy all these realms with Sue, albeit in the context of my own shifting, evolving role as researcher-writer, and any texts that emerge from our collaboration move through and within these spaces as well. Sharon Crowley opens her afterword to *Rhetorical Bodies* with these words from Judith Butler:

> I could not fix bodies as simple objects of thought. . . . [They] tend to indicate a world beyond themselves, but this movement beyond their own boundaries, a movement of boundary itself, appeared to be quite central to what bodies "are." (qtd. in Crowley and Selzer 358)

Our collaboration encapsulates Butler's musings and further exemplifies a unique tension: in both Sue and Glenn we find a set of concrete expectations or relational rules, as well as a contradictory surrender to the inexplicable, to a gut sense or force that exceeds capture. These tensions, both practical and conceptual, exist around a material body—the text for Glenn and her own physical body for Sue—and they are about method: *what I do, how I think about* this body (or this text) that is mine. In the context of my role as researcher-writer, these tensions represent a coming-into-agency, into an identity and methodology defined by movement and uncertainty and by my own material experience as witness.

And yet: "text" as an idea and as a thing brings with it impasse and resistance. In his wonderfully hybridized piece "The Nervous System," Richard Miller reminds us, "As seductive as it is to say that all the world is a text . . . 'discourse' and 'the body,' 'language' and 'lived experience' are neither identical nor interchangeable terms" (269). Miller's brave exploration of his father's suicide attempt in this essay serves as an exploratory, narrative lever for investigating "writing that matters" (278) and a synthesis between traditionally "personal" and "academic" writing. At the same time, Miller illustrates the very material roadblocks to translating, reading, or rendering "lived experience" in words. At stake in this pairing is a reductive dichotomy Miller urges us to resist:

> On the one hand, then, we have the scene in the garage with the knives and the hammer, the rescue workers on their way, the ultimately inaccessible, illegible event. On the other, the speaker at the podium, the performance of a masterful reading, the laughing crowd, the erasure of lived experience, the claim to possess truly useful knowledge. To stage the debate in this way, however, is both to establish a familiar set of oppositions and to guarantee an equally familiar outcome. (266)

As an alternative, Miller describes the process of writing a personally reflective poem—about the first house he lived in—during which he was overcome with emotion. This experience, for Miller, functions as "an I. A. Richard's phrase, a machine to feel with" (273). Such "machinery" becomes for Miller a way into other kinds of analysis, "to think about a host of problems related to 'composition,' broadly construed as the art of putting oneself and one's writing together" (273).

The field of rhetoric-composition currently has much to offer what is Miller's ultimate call—"the process of composing is ever to serve the function of generating hope"—since the 1996 publication of "The Nervous System" (282). While Miller ends his essay with an argument for pedagogical approach that values listening, hearing, and being heard over simply being "seen" in name via traditional kinds of writing and publication, current work in multimodal composing and queer rhetorics pushes us to imagine composing as a far more radical act of rendering than Miller's essay allows. I would argue that the most productive tension and thus chasm in Miller's essay is this "hope" for cohesiveness, "putting oneself and one's writing together," despite what he admits is the "illegible" status of lived experience. Indeed these two, self and text, do not always fit together, even as we find ourselves always dependent on rhetoric, on words and signs to convey as closely as we can a desire to be heard and understood. Miller describes his father's failed effort to explain to emergency medical workers the "tools"—kitchen knives and a hammer—he had gathered for his suicide attempt:

> Then, amidst the frenzied activity in the Intensive Care Unit, my father struggled to explain the presence of the hammer. At a loss for words, he could only say that he had felt at the time that it "might have been of some use." (265)

Miller notes the "relative inaccessibility of this logic," and I would subsequently point at two layers of such inaccessibility: the failure or "misfit" of tools, represented by the uselessness of the hammer in a suicide attempt, as well as the failure or misfit of words themselves in conveying extraordinary psychic pain. The argument that I am making throughout this book—and attempting to embody in the shifting nature of this text—is that we must work in this space of "misfit" and that indeed we must ourselves become "misfits." Such a status evolves from DeVault and Gross's call, for in this process we are reshaped, remade in ways that refuse the traditional contours of proscribed roles. Our humanness problematizes not only our work but who we are in the work. Indeed, amid such disconnect, we encounter new opportunities for knowledge making. We can learn something about both our tools and our pain: why they refuse each other at a certain juncture, why we try again and again to make them sync, why we long for such a vehicle, what we might achieve anyway, and—most importantly—who we become in the trying and failing.

Losing Structure: Movement into the Unexpected

Peter Smagorinsky's much-read, heavily cited essay is valued by social scientific researchers in rhetoric-composition for its inherent generosity: the essay is an effort on the part of a prolific scholar and editor to demystify the process.[2] Indeed Smagorinsky makes a sweeping, revealing effort to help: here is what works; here is where scholars fail; here is how aspiring scholars can get their qualitative research published. And in fact we all want to start our work with the best chance for success, whatever that might mean to us and whatever our disciplinary slants. In the first months of our work and in collaboration with Sue, I aimed to outline boundaries for our project, as I discussed in the opening chapter, which marked a structural effort to establish mutuality and transparency in our work and in the particular moves I was making as a researcher. This was, for me, an enactment of methodological ethics as much as an effort to demystify my own practical steps of doing the research.

Ultimately, however, our collaboration was a collision of lived experience and a desire for, as Miller notes, "writing that matters." This desire was a mix of our differing standpoints and needs, our diverse and respective relationships with writing. Most fundamental, I would argue, is that our collaboration models the impossibility of any sort of easy, dichotomous relationship between what Miller calls "writing that matters in the therapeutic sense" and "writing that matters in the academic sense," with the former affirming "the writer's need for the world" and the latter "the world's need for the writer" (278). Further yet, I would add that this failed dichotomy is not only one of writing and "text" but also one of subjective, methodological "becoming": in fact in our methods, too, we might find a rich collision, a mismatch, between how we learn, how we find out, how we collect data, and even what we might call data in this complex current around the need for words in the urgent, inexplicable context of living and dying. Later in this chapter I will offer one method for engaging such mismatch and for looking reflexively at either side of the disconnect.

In part some of this reflexive work is rooted in the researcher-writer's willingness to embrace self-investigation as an inseparable component of knowledge making. This concept is certainly not new to feminist discussions of methodology, and yet we must constantly reengage what is, in practice, a steep challenge, particularly when we come up against the sort of mismatch Miller describes.[3] Rose's Glenn continues to be instructive here as well. That Glenn can be concurrently lazy, rule abiding, rule dismissing, intuitive, and also deliberative about revising his work because he is "interested in [his] own mind" suggests a potentially rich failure of methodology in exchange for personal growth. Glenn occasions the opportunity to investigate the mismatch between what he "knows" (never end with a quotation) and what he might learn (his own mind). For Halberstam, such an approach privileges those forms of knowledge that are typically "disqualified, rendered nonsensical or nonconceptual or 'insufficiently elaborated'" by status quo methods (11). Halberstam explains:

> Really imaginative ethnographies, for example, depend upon an unknowing relation to the other. To begin an ethnographic project with a goal, with an object of research and a set of presumptions, is already to stymie the process of discovery; it blocks one's ability to learn something that exceeds the frameworks with which one enters. (12)

In dismissing his own framework Glenn opens multiple possibilities for learning: Why might the rule he already knew not work in this case? What is it about his "own mind" that is inaccessible if the rule is applied? Perhaps more profoundly, Glenn's rejection of his framework makes room for Halberstam's "unknowing relation to the other," at least to the extent that suddenly we might search for the source of Glenn's inherited rule. Who is this authoritative other? What motivated the original proclamation of her/his/their rule? And why now this disconnect for Glenn?

In my collaboration with Sue, we routinely came up against either our own or the other's desire for—or resistance to—certainty, the rules we had inherited and that brought us comfort, predictability. This is as much a phenomenon of journeying through terminal illness as it is, I would argue, one of research and writing methodologies that seek to engage and explore such an experience. In explaining to me her experience of others' needs around her perpetually vulnerable terminal status, Sue noted,

Some people just need this for their own sanity: she's cured. It's done. You know what I mean? Because it's like they can't imagine something so uncontrollable and stealth and unpredictable, with no rhyme or reason, could just pop up like that. (Maute, personal interview, 24 Mar. 2014)

From a methodological perspective and from a human one, we all take comfort in certainty. We are grateful for Smagorinsky's blueprint, his recipe for success. However, in the case of my collaboration with Sue, what she describes as a failure of imagination in "something so un-controllable and stealth and unpredictable" marks an inability to know her. "Unknowing" her, to draw on Halberstam, meant treading out into the dark imagination where she resided with that which was not cured but also not immediately measurable: her cancer and its status as terminal, her body for all its abilities despite this diagnosis, the lurking likelihood that ultimately this disease would destroy her, the utterly ungraspable sense of time and rationality, of how or when or why. To know Sue was to take in her unknowns, the fact of her living questions and spaces, to filter these into our talk and writing. Commenting on her own practice of surrender and following this discussion of others' need to hear she was "cured," Sue insisted that her goal instead was to "let go of the outcome" (Maute, personal interview, 24 Mar. 2014). Such an objective is, of course, no objective at all in terms of Smagorinsky's prescription for success.

Impossible Learning: A Method for Not-Knowing

As both Glenn and Sue exemplify, in this letting go we may find new knowledge and new ways to identify within our work. Lisa Mazzei's work in educational research offers a substantive, compelling example of a deconstructive approach to qualitative research in order to, as Mazzei explains, "exploit the blindness and silence created within the context of my research towards a more fruitful discourse at the edges of its boundaries" (*Inhabited Silence* 6). Mazzei embarked initially to study white teachers' attitudes about race, recording and transcribing a series of group interviews. Mazzei describes her early process as follows:

I questioned whether what I had gathered was in fact "thin data." Further examination, however, began to suggest that what I was faced with was not "thin data," but rather an inherited limitation implied in a conventional understanding of the doing of research. In other

words, I was constrained within the boundaries of what had traditionally been considered to count as "data." An attachment to my learned
understanding of "data" had predisposed me to focus on what was per-
ceived as the primary text (spoken word) rather than a consideration
of empirical materials that transgressed traditional boundaries. (65)

Cheryl Glenn's work in rhetorical silences speaks clearly to the impasse
Mazzei discovers in her own work; however, for Mazzei, trained in the
traditional methods Smagorinsky describes, the methodological process
is simply not designed to register silence.[4] Thus in Mazzei's project, "this
silence was experienced as absent of meaning; it was not voiced so was
therefore Other to my purpose" (72).

Mazzei's project ultimately became a radical one in her effort to resist
the "binary of spoken text and silent emptiness." As traditional practices of reading transcripts for patterns and categories had presented
a "troubling resistance" where "voice modulations were lost, as were
the pauses, the sighs," Mazzei redesigned her approach "to develop a
process for listening" (79). With this move, Mazzei acknowledged "the
layers, the complexities, and the contradictions" and listened to her transcripts without reading along, taking notes instead as she heard pauses,
omissions, and intriguing phrases and charting her own impulse to ask
questions of the conversation (80). Using her notes to then "develop an
organizational framework that might guide me in listening to the tapes
again," Mazzei ultimately was able to listen for "the multiple layers of
meaning" and to raise questions about her methodological process, her
positionality, and her expectations for her research (81). Still, this careful
process comes with the risk of greater uncertainty, as Mazzei warns:
"We must be leery of forcing the silences to say what we want them to
say so that we hear what we want to hear" (98). The goal instead is in
fact to identify, to "know" the spaces without filling them "with our
own voice" (98). Such a practice resonates clearly with Halberstam's call
for an "unknowing relation to the other" (12).

Mazzei's willingness to come into contact with what was, essentially,
empty space marked a move into a methodological process that not
only drove the work toward increasing complexity (and potential in-
conclusiveness) but forced Mazzei back on herself. This is work that
engages the researcher as a participant in ways that generate significant
instability in the work itself. This instability takes root, I would argue,
in a self-consciousness that reveals new layers of understanding and
analysis. Mazzei explains:

To engage a problematic of silence in the doing of interviews is to begin the process of *listening to ourselves listening*. . . . For example, in the previous chapter I included an entry from my research journal that expressed my hesitation and even fear at hearing myself, listening to myself as one being researched, and wondering what I might let slip in the silences that were heretofore unknown and unheard by me. (91)

The "hesitation" and "fear" Mazzei describe here suggest a subjectivity that stands to deepen the "mess" of the research even as it offers yet another layer of meaning. This concept, "mess," is one I use with affection, and I pull it from Mazzei herself:

When voice begins to exercise this excessive "messiness," we need to recognize how quickly we move to contain it. The desire to contain or to tame voice is so often couched in the "right" translation that is appropriate and safe. (107)[5]

Of course, that we have some sense of "right"—in any discipline—speaks to the sorts of rules and structures we inherit and to which we often subscribe even unknowingly. As Rose's Glenn reminds us, we have learned these dictums "somewhere along the line," even as we might not understand or believe in the practical application (*Writer's Block* 63). And should we be interested in our "own minds," we must be willing at times to also leave them, to "step out and analyze," as Sue says of her own status as betwixt and between.

Our failures to believe are often ushered in by a crisis of sorts, a project that does not go as planned but that nevertheless opens us to a new sort of faith in method and its potential outcomes. Mazzei describes this well in her discussion of a "troubled listening," one that works "against the categories we create" and that in turn invites us to "acknowledge the limits of language and attempt a listening and asking that confronts these limits" (*Inhabited Silence* 110). Essentially the "outcome" of such work is the discovery of limits, not the arrival at any sort of resolution. Such limits are rich as they teach us about possibility even as they are ever indeterminate. Mazzei explains the outcome of her "deconstructive methodology" further:

It is to open up the possibility of a blank space, not one that is empty, but one that is overflowing with the fullness of absence. And while this space of writing, of research, of writing about research is already disciplined, I seek an undisciplining. (114)

Implicit in Mazzei's caution that we not assign static meaning to silence, that we be wary of the impulse to "discipline" it with what we want to hear, is a kind of endless motion of possibilities for meaning. In other words, if we can allow for "blank spaces" in our work, which I might think of as an analytical tracing of limits, a way of acknowledging what we do not in fact "know," we also make space for research and writing into rhetorical practices that ultimately connect us to each other despite chasms we can't traverse: living and dying, healthy and ill.

Making Method in Dark Spaces

> The process is you take all your data, you transcribe all these interviews, you take all your artifacts, you know the written texts and everything . . . and then you figure out . . . what do I have here? But what does it mean to say, well, I can't figure this out by myself? I have all this stuff but I can't really even figure it out by myself. (Restaino in Maute, personal interview, 24 Mar. 2014)

So much of my experience as journey partner and researcher involved contending with my own limitations. I found myself surrounded by what we might call "data" while simultaneously engulfed in one of the most powerful relationships of my life. I could not separate this relationship from the rhetorical artifacts it generated. As it was all born of dialogue, written and spoken, I felt the need for continued dialogue in order to understand all that surrounded me. Of course, the underbelly of this desire is its ultimate impossibility: not only would death halt our rolling conversation, but in fact lived, bodily experience itself was an inevitable dividing line between us. I want to flesh out the implications of this tension more fully to open a way into method that responds directly to such uncertainty. The conviction that I could not do this alone—"this" being to make sense of Sue's terminal illness in words—matters and remains unchanged. I continue to hold this conviction even as I go forward indeed now alone. In fact I go forward in this way in order to exemplify not only the reality of such limitation but also its unique value to feminist rhetorical study; it is a thing in itself. This paradox becomes a way of seeing both of us, our desires and our losses, and *in this very seeing* also becomes a vehicle for methodological thinking and a way to do the work.

Sue and I each presented a contradiction unique to our circumstances. When I implored her for direction regarding what I should do with the many very personal artifacts we had accumulated, asked her what my response should be in the event one of her children might, when older and searching for more information, ask for audio recordings or transcripts or writing samples, her response was, "I'd want them to know their mother. Just nothing that would hurt anyone." Again, this desire to be known and yet not to hurt is at once deeply human and implicitly contradictory. In fact, often knowing comes with pain: knowledge and enlightenment usher in at least some disappointment. My positioning as writer, researcher, the one who remains, is underinformed. I operate with only partial directions; I must make decisions based upon her contradictory desires. Further, my own conviction that I need her with me in order to make sense of things, to help me figure out what it all means or what to *do*, is bound up here as well. In certain ways Sue could not—or would not—clarify things for me when she had the opportunity, like when I specifically asked her to tell me what to do with our many primary source materials. Similarly, she also could not ever get me to a place of full comprehension of her bodily or emotional experience of terminal breast cancer in words. Though we found ourselves on an island together, I never wore her shoes. I could not.

In a sense, this project's refusal of full clarity—either understanding in words or in body Sue's lived experience and in the denial of direction—puts me, as researcher and writer, on display in ways that are fundamental to understanding this work.[6] I am exposed for what and who I am: partial, half of, incomplete, not fully coherent. In her memoir of teaching in Austria, Sondra Perl recounts a transformative relationship with one of her students, Margret, whose status as a descendant of Nazi sympathizers ultimately forces Perl to confront her own experience of growing up Jewish in the 1950s in the wake of the Holocaust. For Perl, the relationship with Margret outlines and ultimately destabilizes her own boundaries, even as it reinforces their very different respective standpoints. Reading Margret's journal for class one evening, Perl is "startled when [she] come[s] across the following words: *I ask you to forgive me*" (198). She goes on to describe the ways in which this experience forces a confrontation with her own limits:

> Margret, I think, has nothing to be forgiven for; my granting forgiveness will be, at best, an empty gesture. But as I read her request, it is as if I am seeing myself for the first time. For what I see is a woman who has always found it impossible to forgive; a young girl who has grown into an adult who has taken pride in condemning the

Germans and has happily maintained that they are all Nazis, making it impossible to see anything else about them; a person so sure of her stand, so confident in her righteousness, she has been blind to any other view. (199)

Margret's gesture forces Perl to know herself more fully—"I am seeing myself for the first time"—and in her attempt to respond Perl not only must confront what have been her limitations thus far but also must feel the pain beneath such boundaries. She explains, "Carefully camouflaged, I nonetheless stood in the world as a woman who bore the burden of betrayal" (199). Finally seeing herself through the camouflage, in a sense, opens a capacity both to hurt and be hurt in ways that are at once profoundly freeing and also reminiscent of what Richard Feynman has called "a deep understanding—the difference between knowing the name of something and knowing something" (*Richard Feynman*).[7]

The notion of "naming" is significant beyond—as Feynman uses it—scientific terminology, research practices, or issues of disciplinary identity. In research, knowledge making, and the process of writing, pressing on the tension between knowing and naming stands to unhinge the security of carefully defined boundaries, allowing us to cross otherwise forbidden lines in the spirit of deep (and thus fraught, incomplete) understanding. Perl's example continues to be instructive. She describes her experience of forgiving Margret, an act she thought initially impossible and unnecessary:

> I notice that the act of granting forgiveness carries great resonance. Words of forgiveness are not mere words spoken into a void. They are performative: speaking them alters me. For once I do, the grip of hatred and righteousness begins to loosen. I begin to feel as though I have shed a layer of my skin, a covering that has encased me and kept me closed. Suddenly I am free to see my past differently, to reinterpret it, and to extend compassion to the young girl who could not accept the world's betrayal of her people. (200)

At work here is of course a deeply personal process of transformation for Perl. However, I want to take an interpretative, analytical risk here and suggest that this very personal process in fact doubles as a methodological model in feminist rhetorical research and in particular in my collaboration with Sue. What Perl bares on the page is a process of being remade in the work. This remaking is subjective, intimate, emotional, and intellectual.

To share space on the page with such uncertainty comes with significant risk, and in her efforts to see Margret and thus herself anew, Perl explains the unique stakes in her move to ask questions and see possibility in ways she had previously forbidden:

> I have feared that raising such questions risks denigrating the memory of the millions who entered the gas chambers or lost their lives in ghettos or in hastily dug unmarked graves. What was taken from them—their lives, their loved ones, the continuity of family—is not forgivable. They remain victims of genocide. (201)

"Such questions" for Perl are the enduring, impossible ones, those made speakable only by the loosening of long-held practices and beliefs, by the act of forgiveness: "But what, then, remains beyond the emptiness? What do those of us who live in its aftermath inherit? What are we to do? How are we to act?" (201). The questions Perl raises are of both method *and* methodology, but they are most importantly questions of identity, posed by and for the doer behind the work. This doer—writer, researcher, thinker, human, Jew, woman—raises new questions that each possess a certain element of bottomlessness. There is, after all, no undoing the "emptiness" that Perl describes. But there is equally no underestimating, for Perl, the urgency of the aftermath—*what are we to do*—nor the possibility inherent in dismantling her own boundaries to comprehension. Radical action and radical thought in this case, I would argue, happen when we follow the threads, to—in a sense—surrender ourselves into these contradictory currents.

Sue's treatment ushered in a particularly poignant opportunity for such radical surrendering. After she received a radiological intervention to her liver that would extend her life by about six months, Sue's orientation to time shifted toward careful celebration of mere days: a good day without physical pain, a day spent around her children. We conducted a long recorded interview following the news from Memorial Sloan Kettering regarding her liver's optimal response, and this interview was nothing short of a celebration between us, filled with laughter and awe. Sue had been in liver failure in the weeks before, her belly swollen with fluid, but—though she continued to rely on a drain to combat this fluid buildup—in the weeks since this treatment her bilirubin levels dropped significantly and the telltale yellowing of her eyes faded. We were ecstatic. We had wept together over her swollen abdomen, the pain and discomfort of it, its glaring indication that something was very wrong. Coming together to reflect on the improvement of the situation was steeped in the miraculous for us both.

Our conversation that day could have rolled on for hours as we marveled over the news, and evidence, of the effectiveness of the treatment. But I had to leave sooner than I wanted as I had a meeting back on campus, and as I hurriedly packed up my recorder and notebook, Sue assured me that we'd "have time" to continue our work. She then told me excitedly that now, with the improvement of her liver function, she could in fact help to coach her daughter's lacrosse team in the spring. In the telling, she also teased me, reminding me that she had mentioned this intention to me on another occasion, one that was indeed dire: when her husband and I had worked together to shave her head. As I gathered her hair up off the kitchen floor, she talked about how she planned to help out with the team, as she had done in past years; I must have looked at her with doubt, clumps of hair in my hands, broom at my side. And so on this day, with this news of her liver's (temporary) resiliency, she joked with me, reminiscing about this earlier moment, accusing me lovingly of having obvious doubts, of nodding back then with much disbelief.

And she was right, of course. In fact I think we both understood the humor in her teasing because we had both felt the unlikelihood in her earlier wish. Following the transcription of our celebratory interview and Sue's joking as I dashed off, I wrote this reflection:

> I realized last night after completing the transcription of our conversation on Monday that I am in an alternate orbit with you. The things we can laugh at are not funny in the real world. Meaning changes even as we toss back and forth words that are all the same, even read for what they are—terminal and morbid and honest and real. And it's normal and they are not so scary. We are in bed with those words, we are living with them, playing with them, rolling them around and propping them up to rest on. (Restaino, "Alternate Orbit")

The easy marriage of horror and play is a rhetoric unique, I would argue, to trauma, which often makes the incomprehensible strangely, disarmingly livable.[8] Psychoanalytic writer Michael Eigen describes the process as one in which "sensitivity is ripped apart by life": "In one or another way, the agonies that sensitivity suffers are tasted or gone through, over and over, a movement toward another place" (722). Trying to capture, even authorize, the morbid humor that hovered between us on good days like the one following Sue's liver news, I go on in my reflection with a tumbling, stumbling effort:

> "And that I'm able to coach Paige's lacrosse team this year . . ." That was good for a laugh that you said that before I thought you never could. Again, joy—how funny—what you said, and I thought you would never be able to, might not even make it, but now you are doing it, and "we have time." How wonderful. On the outside this is so sad. Outsiders weep through this terrible tragedy. (Restaino, "Alternate Orbit")

Fundamental to my reflection here is the slippery, jumbled rhetorical quality of the words themselves—"what you said, and I thought you would never be able to, might not even make it"—which move in a way that emphasizes disconnection, a lack of interrelatedness or cause and effect. One phrase doesn't necessarily justify or explain the other, though they follow each other. At root, too, is of course contradiction: joy and sorrow, comedy and tragedy are strange yet comfortable bedfellows; "we are in bed with those words." I remember distinctly the feeling of my own puzzlement over the degree of security or familiarity I felt within and among the "words," by which I mean the threatening, looming ideas or themes that threaded through our collaboration. While I often experienced sadness, I also experienced great joy—on a day that came with good news, for example—and in either case this movement between sadness and joy was rhythmic, mostly predictable for quite a while. The reality, though, was that embedded, buried perhaps, in that increasing rhythmic ease was a parallel, growing shock, a pending unpredictability or surprise. In fact the body would ultimately reach its demise; in fact good days would eventually disappear entirely; in fact "gone" is indeed really gone. I'm reminded again of Hawhee's analysis of an ancient wrestling manual:

> The opponent's moves and the attention to specificity they require introduce difference to the repetition, demanding a new move in between each of the throwing directives. Stylistically, the manual captures the difference between repetitions, demanding and producing its own kind of rhythmic response. ("Bodily Pedagogies" 149)

Our participation in a rhythm ensures our vulnerability to its disruption, our sensitivity to shifts; and the more facile we become at following these movements and anticipating them, the more incomprehensible the upending of our reliable frameworks.

Richard Miller refers to such tension as the "inevitable gnarl of contradiction that results . . . when the personal and the academic are set loose and allowed to interrogate one another with no predetermined outcome" (284). We experience a disorienting "bleeding into": what we have come to know or define as impermeable, unchanging, reveals faulty or weaker boundaries, loose or unclean edges. Surrendering into such a reality is oftentimes all, indeed the very best, we can do with what we have before us. In fact it was in the transcript of our discussion about the positive, temporary response of Sue's liver that she claimed her goal was "to let go of the outcome," which indeed mirrors Miller's projections as well. This orientation was significant to our collaboration more broadly, to our friendship, to our being able to keep doing what we were doing as both a research and a living-through process, and for numerous reasons. In particular, "letting go of the outcome" made documenting and sharing Sue's experience possible. We did not have to offer a static rationale for the work, to fit it or name it in any identifiable way, nor did we have to look so far ahead—*what does this all mean? where might this all go?*—that any given moment itself became irrelevant or at least less significant. Our needs often moved back and forth: at times to understand or explain, at times to comfort, at times to mourn, at times to celebrate. There was ample room for Benjamin's "third," which I explored at greater length earlier in this book, where the question "'Who created this rhythm, you or I?'" lingers unanswered as we reveal ourselves to, and are revealed by, the other. The result then is a collection of words and more importantly a process—data, rhetorical artifacts in motion with each other—that are unpredictable, not necessarily linear, at times contradictory and unstable, and indeed perhaps on a course for total failure. For Miller, it's in this relinquishing of a predetermined outcome, as in the merger of the personal and the academic, that "a different kind of 'writing that matters' is getting produced":

> a kind of writing that seeks, as Foucault himself sought in revising his project on the history of sexuality, "to learn to what extent the effort to think one's own history can free thought from what it silently thinks, and so enable it to think differently." (284)

My effort here to put into words that which, in essence, did not make logical sense, like morbidity/humor and death/hope, indeed is "a kind of writing" that performs or embodies its very message or meaning. Here we might make space in text for, as Miller writes, "a place to see and re-see the components and possible trajectories of one's lived experience and to situate and re-situate that experience within a world of other thoughts and embedded reactions" (285). Indeed in Miller's father we find this very phenomenon: the gathering of a tool (the hammer) that, by its very material, functional insufficiency, illustrates the unspeakable, incomprehensible scope of his pain. We are complex, faulty, incoherent researchers, writers, thinkers, and humans.

Working within the "gnarl of contradiction," to draw again on Miller's language, yields that which Miller refers to as "the very thing the academy is most in need of" (285). Indeed, despite the years that have passed since the publication of "The Nervous System," Miller's prescription of need strikes me as more urgent and more pressing than ever: "a technology for producing and sustaining the hope that tomorrow will be better than today and that it is worth the effort to see to it that such hopes aren't unfounded" (285). Of course such a need is profound, urgent, and difficult to satisfy in the context of terminal illness; surely for Sue and me the desire to find hope in the face of her progressing illness was a constant drive behind our collaboration. However, I want to also suggest that hope—as a need of "the academy," according to Miller—has a special role in how we write and do research. In certain kinds of work, such hope takes root in the failure of "answerable questions," to remember Smagorinsky, as well as in the process of "unknowing," as Halberstam instructs us. I do not insist that we necessarily seek this phenomenon in all the work that we do but rather that we make it possible, pay attention, recognize, and respond to opportunities to "'free thought from what it silently thinks, and so enable it to think differently'" (R. Miller 284). Such freeing can take "technological" form, as Miller suggests, which I imagine as a set of tools, equipment we can use in new or unexpected ways to generate similarly new, perhaps even unrecognizable thinking, methods, and texts (and thus hope). This work reaches into us: we must remember that as we are the makers and users of tools, the subject itself—our sense of identity, purpose, drive—is potentially set free as well when we engage Miller's mismatch, the jagged work of "putting oneself and one's writing together" (273). It's here, once again, where we stand to become productive misfits.

Making Room for Hope: A Technology for Not-Knowing

In March 2016 I offered a workshop as part of the Coalition of Feminist Scholars in the History of Rhetoric and Composition's "Action Hour," an event at the Conference on College Composition and Communication.[9] In a published version of this workshop, making the materials available to others for use, I explain my inspiration behind the practice of the "reverse interview":

> No sooner did I approach the early days of our collaboration with a plan and a frame, the structure was overturned by the dynamics of our relationship and deepening love, by the growing threat of Sue's illness, by the unknown, intangible quality of dying itself. Together we shared an urgent need to make meaning in words and to understand this drive in our unique context. (Restaino, "Performing Feminist Action")

The workshop itself attempted to put Mazzei's "troubled listening" into practice, taking participants through the process of generating a reflective text as interviewers/researchers—data in itself—that charted their reactions, questions, and hesitations in response to interviewee feedback. Such exploratory writing on the part of the researcher ideally should happen during the process of listening to audio recordings, a kind of free-write response to hearing the dialogue as it unfolds, interrupting that dialogue with insight, observation, and further questions. In my workshop, I proposed a second layer of collaborative, written reflection, which invites the researcher and participant to review together the interviewer/researcher's reactions to the audio recording and to add further questions, connections, and insights to the reflective text. This generates a kind of "reverse interview" where researcher and participant work together to understand the interviewer/researcher's initial responses to interview data, the impact of those responses on the interviewer/researcher, and the extent to which such responses might point at larger issues of connection or disconnect on either side of the research process. It's here, I would argue, that we might come close to generating the sort of data that invites a version of Miller's "writing that matters." In occasioning an intersection between the personal—potentially on either side of the research relationship—and the academic, we stand to learn more about how we construct meaning and how we are shaped by each other as we try to work toward new understandings. I would also argue that such a practice destabilizes the inherent hierarchy of the researcher/collaborator relationship, making the researcher vulnerable to the research participant in ways aligned with rigorous feminist practice.

In my collaboration with Sue, I did not have a script or plan to follow of the sort I imagined nearly two years following her death for the workshop. But I routinely found myself without direction, in foreign territory, and in a sense some large piece of the work involved a willing-ness to follow the uncertainty itself: What would this illness do next? How might our interview and writing about it matter? What kind of "interview" involves just pressing "record" and following a conversation wherever it might lead? Where do I find myself up against the limits of what I can understand? Paired though with such uncertainty was a clar-ity of connection and need: for reasons that exceeded my understanding or even control, Sue and I both felt driven to move through it together.

My responses to navigating this strange, contradictory mix of feel-ings were to share what I could of it with Sue during our conversations and also to write reflectively and routinely about my experience in our collaboration. This writing is its own body of data, beyond our tran-scripts or any writing Sue did as part of our work, and often contends with what I experienced as the material and conceptual inaccessibility of terminal illness. Indeed, this arena is where our pursuit of rational-ity or logic in words simply cowers beneath the shadow of the failing body, or—as with Miller's father—the enormity of psychic pain. That such tension might play out "in text" breathes hope toward the very "writing that matters" that Miller imagines, even as it underscores the limits of what we can fully communicate. On one occasion, in fact just about exactly four weeks before her passing, I showed up at Sue's house, and she insisted we go for a walk. This experience of walking with her, sick as she was at that point, had me buckling emotionally as I faced her physical weakness, the body that had once been an athletic force to be reckoned with. Afterward I wrote to describe this experience, to capture it, and found I could barely offer much commentary or insight. But what I did offer Sue—in the moment and which I described in my written reflection—speaks to my own futile turning to words, to the generation of text, as a solution or response to that which far exceeded my control. I quote my reflection at some length:

> You wanted to walk. *I have to move, Jess. Look at my legs. They are so skinny, wasting away. Let's go.*
>
> And we did. We walked—as you wanted—all the way to the lake, one mile there, you told me. Slow but steady. And our destination, as you chose for us: a gazebo on the edge of a small beach, staring out onto the water. My breath caught when you hesitated—one step up, falter, wait, rock, second step up. And then we sat. . . .
>
> In truth you never whine. You don't. But you did have your strong positions yesterday, sitting by the lake, that spot hard-earned: changes

to the town over time, the problems of too much money, summer as riding bikes and staying put, having everything "right here" . . .

I said—Listen—you know—I've got enough material to write a book at this point, and I will, but—if you have things to say, if you've got some stuff going on up there that you want to get out, if you want to go *on the record*, you know . . . I'm your girl. I'll show up with my recorder and my notebook and you can just go for it.

I want to. I want to, especially with what I'm going through. ("Reflection: Walk to Lake")

We would generate more writing after this moment, but it would be her last wishes, directions for her services, tasks she wanted completed, a message for her family. It would not be another of our recorded, transcribed conversations, nor would she write more for me to read in any formal way. We would, of course, keep writing back and forth until her death—text messages, updating each other and asking for/about the other, planning and responding—but these messages often just served to help us find each other, in spirit or in body: *I'll be there; I'm on my way; I'm sorry this is happening; I'm here.*

I want to make the paradoxical claim then that at this dire point, at this moment where the reality of dying seemed to undermine our ability to understand or to intellectualize, Sue and I both expressed a contradictory desire for our formal "academic" process. I offered to bring back the recorder and notebook; she responded, "I want to, especially with what I'm going through." We are suddenly, in a sense, together wielding a hammer in a suicide attempt. Richard Miller quotes Foucault's "rhetorical question": "'What is at stake in the will to truth . . . in the will to utter this "true" discourse, if not desire and power?'" (270). Terminal illness is an exercise in powerlessness in many ways, and that we might experience material words, the generation of "text," as a salve to our very vulnerability, our helplessness in the face of the gigantic, exposes our hope that there is some sort of other way, some kind of alternative to the otherwise inevitable failure of the physical. We must become writers and researchers of a new order, one born of a faith that the generation of "writing that matters," to draw again on Miller—impossible as it ever was (and still is) to write and talk our way to full understanding—might deliver us beyond our relative smallness. It's here, I would argue, that we might find that deep tension, Miller's "inevitable gnarl of contradiction," where new knowledge, new ways of doing research and of writing, might take root and emerge (284). Here we find a humbled, self-aware power we so desire (and fear). And so, I will end with a quotation—one that emerges from the philosopher Martin Buber's musings on therapeutic method—as Rose's Glenn remembers *never* to do, in hopes that it just might work:

> In certain cases a therapist is terrified by what he is doing because he begins to suspect that at least in such cases, but finally perhaps, in all, something entirely other is demanded of him—something incompatible with the economics of his profession, dangerously threatening indeed to his regulated practice of it. What is demanded of him is that he draw the particular case out of the role of professional superiority, achieved and guaranteed by long training and practice into the elementary situation between one who calls and one who is called. The abyss does not call to his competently functioning security of action, but to the abyss that is to the self of the doctor, that selfhood that is hidden under the structures erected through training and practice, that is itself encompassed by chaos, itself familiar with demons, but is graced with the humble power of wrestling and overcoming and is ready to wrestle and overcome, thus, ever anew. (Buber 94)

BLOODWORK
(A TEXT MESSAGE)

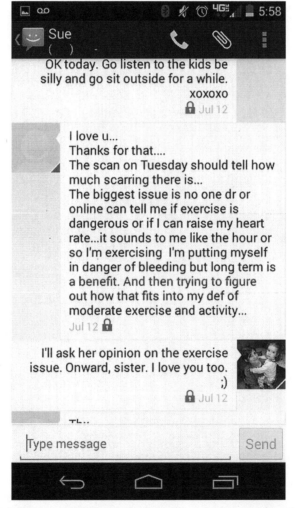

Sue weighs the risks versus the benefits of exercise. *Restaino and Maute, text message correspondence, 12 July 2014.*

STAGE I
RADICAL CARE
RHETORICAL BODIES IN CONTACT

Think of how we would have to orient to illness. We could no longer assume, for example, that this or that illness is known by its diagnostic label, that the clinical path of disease is what matters most, that asthma is asthma, that diverticulitis is diverticulitis. We would have to unname the illness and study the complexity, the subjectivity, and the variability of different people's lives. Of course, the point of this unnaming exercise would not be to let go of all the progress made in medical science. To understand people's experience we would need to get really close to them so that their hopes become our hopes, their pain becomes our pain— we would need to listen and speak, read and write in a manner that is attentive to the things of the world that are ultimately unnamable. Our words would now have to be "as slow, as new, as single, and as tentative" as if we were going down a path away from the familiar toward a world we had never navigated before.

—*Max Van Manen, "The Pathic Nature of Inquiry and Nursing"*

In July, the month before her death, Sue suffered from internal bleeding and, in her liver, portal vein hypertension. These conditions proved not only frightening but deadly: the poor function of her liver caused starvation as nutrients could not be distributed to the rest of her body. The failure of blood flow through the portal vein caused smaller tributaries to pick up some of the work, and this work was too taxing for such small streams, causing erosion and internal bleeds. The most frightening of these occurred in her esophagus, causing her to vomit blood and need a transfusion. Externally, her muscles wasted visibly: legs that were once fast and fierce became spindly. Her sneakers appeared oversized at the base of legs worn so thin. Together we tried to reorient to her changing body, to find new words and new ways of thinking about it. This was a process at once grief-filled and sprinkled with anxious hope: maybe there was some small bit of exercise she could do on good days; perhaps there wouldn't be another bad bleed; maybe a belt could support her swollen abdomen and make movement more comfortable.

None of these medical afflictions is extraordinary in the space of terminal breast cancer. No oncologist would be surprised by this progression of disease. Still I often privately, desperately consulted a good friend, a colon-rectal surgeon, about the growing threats associated with Sue's liver. "I'm sorry, Jess, but she is dying. I know it's hard to lose a best friend," would be her compassionate, educated response. Though I understood these efforts at honesty as an extension of care for me, I struggled to believe in Sue's decline. And for a while she did, too. And though we both staged periodic protests, ultimately we moved into understanding together, gathered around her body to see, feel, and hear its visible declarations of failure. In this chapter, I want to explore this "gathering around" as a kind of rhetoric that exceeds earlier feminist notions of care and that demands instead radical sharing, at once threatening and comforting, housed in materiality. While such a material transaction finds its scholarly roots in rhetorics of embodiment, phenomenology of illness, and, most recently, Shannon Walters's work on rhetorical touch, my goal in this chapter is to push the focus toward a consideration of research and writing more broadly. Specifically, what can we learn about how we perform the work of writing and research when we enact bodily care? What is it that our bodies—in communicative contact—can uniquely teach us about knowledge making? How might our bodies generate data or, at least, in what ways might the handling of and care for our bodies teach us about how to handle the diverse data we collect and write about as scholars who study rhetoric? How might this handling and care be a feminist rhetorical practice?

Shannon Walters begins *Rhetorical Touch* with a meditation on Helen Keller's relationship to touch, acknowledging that such contact was both lifeblood and scourge. Quoting Keller, Walters points at a necessary synthesis process unique to the physical: "'Into the tray of one's consciousness are tumbled thousands of scraps of experience. . . . I put together my pieces this way and that, but they will not dovetail properly'" (26). Indeed, overcoming this "dismemberment" required helping hands in the form of Keller's longtime teacher, Anne Sullivan, and others to "[sort] through the fragments, literally cutting with scissors and pasting them together 'into a proper linear narrative'" (27). Of course, Sullivan's language—"'into a proper linear narrative'"—here hints at the impossible: so few narratives are neatly linear. Perhaps more importantly, Sullivan's move to assemble Keller's "pieces" ultimately ignited all kinds of public distrust around Keller's texts and her abilities. For Walters the significance—and also the taboo—of touch itself becomes most meaningful, opening space to explore the rhetorical nature of touch in "engender[ing] a partnership and reciprocal interaction of emotion among people with disabilities and their audiences, facilitating identification" (145).

Such identification, however, is not certain or even necessarily stable, and surely touch itself comes with the threat of harm or misuse. Walters does not argue that rhetorical touch is a seamless pathway to understanding between parties. It is, instead, a *dynamis*, one that ushers in "radical complexity and uncertainty" and that makes possible our "aptitude for working at the edges of language" (199). This aptitude involves, I would argue, a capacity to value connection *and* disconnection. In other words, bodies in contact are simultaneously porous and distinct, each feeling and affecting the other. Touch teaches us that there are limits to what we can understand and experience. As Cynthia Lewiecki-Wilson writes of metonymy, "The paradox that identity includes non-identity within it: I may be like you in some ways, share some associations, but I am not like you in other ways" (qtd. in Walters 201). As Walters notes, bodies in contact hold a similar tension.

Terminal illness and its necessity for physical care open radical space in which bodies—healthy and ill—must come together across difference. As a friend, I took care of Sue's body in ways that emphasized the differences between us. But as someone who occupies a body that is similarly composed, that has the potential, of course, to become ill, that feels pain, there were ways in which that care also brought me closer into understanding. As a research collaborator on the outside of Sue's terminal illness, I must contend with and examine the ways in which our bodies, in their unique relationship to each other, pushed and pulled us both into and out of comprehension. This is intimate, even radical rhetorical work but—to the extent we might think of the physical body as "data" generating, as Walters's work supports—also instructive for how we approach such work and the more expansive possibilities for the *dynamis*, to draw again on Walters, of the research collaboration. In order to work through these possibilities more fully, I want to sketch out here the alternating needs Sue and I each brought into our collaboration for which touch was the experiential crux for our shared rhetoric, what we could each understand about the other and what we could not. By using the term "needs" I am working from the fundamental standpoint that the need to communicate and understand is a human one and that, as "symbol using animals," we draw on the body as one means by which to articulate such an overarching need.[1] There are three areas of need that I see as centrally important in the context of the embodied researcher-participant *dynamis*:

1. I (participant) need you (researcher) to feel this in your body so you can understand.
2. I (researcher) need to feel that I can't understand your (participant) experience.
3. I (participant) need you (researcher) to take care of my body so I (as represented by the body) am safe and valued.

While I will give careful attention to all three in what follows, I want to focus briefly here on the third for the sake of further context. I am inclined to think of the body itself as a "body of data," what we might generate in any typical research collaboration, though often in more traditional textual forms: interview transcripts, field notes, textual artifacts. The body in terminal illness becomes a uniquely observable, shifting physical phenomenon, one linked to the passage of time more powerfully than perhaps any other corpus. But this notion of "observation," in the traditional research context, is of course a potentially problematic one, as the experience of being observed takes on added and ever more dangerous significance when the body's vulnerability is so exposed. Phenomenologist Max Van Manen writes of "the objectifying medical look" and the extent to which serious illness illuminates for us "the object-like nature of our body" (14, 12). It is this capacity for object status that also imbues the terminally ill body with its radical potential to destabilize this objectifying distance, to connect self and other to the meaning and raw vulnerability rooted in such a circumstance. But here is where some of the deepest challenge rests: How do we take good care of the most vulnerable bodies? What happens when the body is defined by the unexpected or by the grotesque? Rooted in the need for safety through bodily care are two tenets about "data": there is no "bad" data, and there is no "unusable" data. Data with repulsive or grotesque qualities must be welcomed and valued in the spirit of collaboration and respect. In rhetorics of terminal illness, all the body brings must have its place in the *dynamis*.

Feminist discussions of "care" have long explored the dangers of essentialized "women's work" as well as the more positive potential for reciprocity and exchange.[2] These discussions remain crucially important, and my argument for the body-in-need as a site of radical care and rhetorical exchange builds on both these dangers and potentialities. We simply cannot escape our bodies. The chaos and destruction that breast cancer enacts on the sexed female body is a unique pain, and our location in any body either gives or denies access to understanding some of this suffering. For Sue and me, our bodies met around a series of shared experiences that at once took me as far into comprehension as I could go and also indicated the line of understanding that, as defined by my own bodily limits, I could not cross. It was through these connections and disconnections that we, together—limited, comprehending, misunderstanding—came to acknowledge and mourn Sue's death. It is perhaps through this yearning for comprehension and connection, and this unique frustration over the ensuing boundary lines, that touch functions most profoundly to communicate that which can't be linguistically articulated. Indeed, we are physically overcome by our powerlessness before the body in its decline.

In his writing on phenomenology and medical care, Max Van Manen describes the transactional power of touch for the ill patient as an opportunity to "re-experience his own skin" following the "broken, disrupted, or disturbed relation with the body" that marks serious illness (8–9). However, beneath this need for reunion or reconnection with the body for the sick lurks an alternate, equally essential physical transaction: the alienation of healthy bodies, those isolated, disempowered "others" who surround the diseased body. Van Manen quotes at painful length Monica Clarke's description of her experience, as a mother, of struggling to assist her young daughter through a serious asthma attack:

> "I pick her up, her arms around my neck. She grips but holds herself away, straining upward and leaning back with the need to have space all around her chest. We go into the kitchen, all blue shadows in the night light. I put her on a high stool, her arms up on a pillow on the kitchen counter. We try the inhaler again. This is wrong, I know. She has already had too much and it is not working.
>
> "Dark curls matted stuck to her forehead, all of her sweaty under my hands. Little shoulders, ribs. Her lips are dark blackish in the

dim kitchen light. I have to decide what to do, but I am empty and stupid. My thoughts fly high above the moment, not touching us, not present. I am outside myself watching the scene that unfolds like a bad movie." (21)

Critical in this description is a twofold reality. The first is Clarke's physically felt comprehension of her daughter's suffering—"'she grips but holds herself away . . . all of her sweaty under my hands'"—which propels meaning, "'This is wrong, I know.'" The second of course is Clarke's clear physical frustration, that of the enforced, tangible boundary between her and her daughter: she cannot, in essence, enter her child's breath and breathe for her. This desperate frustration dislocates her from her own body: "'I am outside myself.'" As the mother of two young girls, as I write this and reflect on Clarke's words, I find myself with quickened breath, feeling my youngest daughter's small ribs beneath my hands, and I resonate uncomfortably with Clarke's maternal panic.[3]

Rhetorical touch in Clarke's narrative exposes the tension between connection and disempowerment, an embodied experience of urgency and understanding laced with an equal sense of impotence, Clarke's ineffectiveness in righting the situation. Earlier in the book I explored Jack Halberstam's notion of failure as an inherently queer practice, and I want to pull this idea forward once again for purposes of affirming the activist potential in rhetorical touch. Halberstam describes the project partly thus: "It is this version of feminism that I seek to inhabit, a feminism that fails to save others or to replicate itself, a feminism that finds purpose in its own failure" (128). Indeed, Clarke's narrative is in every way an enactment of such a feminism: she is neither savior nor "one" with her daughter's body and experience. She must struggle fruitlessly against her own edges, her own demarcated lines; she is denied full power. Forced to accept this denial, she must acknowledge that the ultimate agency lies outside of her, in her daughter's body: "Her eyes fill to cry and I am there living in my anger and my fear. 'Stop that, don't cry, just breathe damn you, breathe?'" (qtd. in Van Manen 21). Reflecting on her side of the experience in their coauthored piece, Clarke's daughter, Sasha, remembers,

> "I always told my Mum that this was the worst one ever but she always said it was just the same as the last time. I never believed her. I used to think she wouldn't say that if she could crawl inside my body right now, but I learned later that she was right. I think it was just because I was so scared. Sometimes I used to cry and that only made it worse, so I stopped." (20)

Sasha then, too, must contend with the impossibility of their sameness. As her mother cannot in fact "crawl inside [her] body right now," Sasha must face the limits of her mother's understanding and power. Sasha thus becomes the agent: "'I used to cry and that only made it worse, so I stopped.'" This need to problem-solve, to claim agency, happens alongside a certain kind of loss: Sasha's mother cannot fully feel what she feels. Our desire for shared feeling, a desire for rhetoric, does not disappear even as we contend with our losses, what we are unable to do or know.

I (participant) need you (researcher) to feel this in your body so you can understand.

As we trace the curve of each other's boundaries, we are in a kind of intimate if frustrating contact. Thus equally profound in Clarke's narrative capacity are the ripples of physical understanding between Clarke and her child and the text's propensity for physical impact on a reading audience. Certainly as a reader I recognize enough of my own physical experience of maternity in Clarke's retelling to have a palpable, bodily reaction to her narrative. It is at these physical crossroads that we find pathways to urgent communications, those that may otherwise prove linguistically inaccessible. The "successful" text is dependent upon rhetorical touch in ways that exceed its very linguistic limits. The rhetorical move into touch is often an expression of the need to confirm the other's ability to understand while simultaneously aware that such understanding likely cannot be communicated in words. Despite this drive toward touch, of course, I would argue that touch carries with it an element of taboo, that it is outside the bounds of what we consider the cognitive work of academic discourse. When we work by hand, we do not use our heads: Walters's depiction of public scrutiny around Keller's dependence on her teacher's assemblage of her "pieces" easily tells us as much, as does Jim Corder's recounting of his grandmother's rendering of quilts composed of scrap material, without pattern or training, by which "without design, she made design" ("I in Mine" 260).[4]

Given the tension that our bodies seem to sustain as beacons of subsequent authority and inferiority, demands on our physical experience can feel invasive and oppressive. Writing about the reception of her work with HIV-positive women, Patti Lather reflects succinctly and with some frustration, "Why the need to know I cried?" (211). Lather refers here to a common question she received from readers who wanted to know whether she was moved to tears by the suffering, and often death, of her research participants. For Lather this "need to know" is born of an "Oprah-ization of this era of confessional talk," and the corresponding "validity of tears" is a source of "great discomfort" (211). While Lather seeks an "undramatized, largely effaced narrative presence" (211), I want to hold the search for tears—a physical response—as a kind of rhetorical yearning, an impulse for human contact of the sort that only a medium that exceeds words can deliver. In this case we might think of tears—not tears of pity but rather of personal loss and grief—as a version of "rhetorical touch," which Walters reminds us "is not necessarily uniquely linguistic or always conveyable in written or spoken form" (13). Of course, Lather's audience might ask out of a seemingly impersonal curiosity, but this too has its place in the search for relatable human experience.

My own experience of being moved to tears in my collaboration with Sue is a fraught one, a challenge to my tendency toward personal privacy and my characteristic difficulty with asking others for help. There was my capacity for crying outside of our relationship—when in conversation with others about Sue's status, or when presenting on the work after her death—and there was my capacity to be moved to tears in the privacy of our relationship, in front of Sue, as her illness progressed. The latter, I would argue, became transitional for us in terms of destabilizing our roles, communicating to Sue not only my ability to understand that she was dying but also my own weakness, my sense of impending loss and need for comfort. This comfort—signaled by the exposure of my tears—became a kind of care she provided me with at the end of her life, essentially inverting our respective authority. The researcher/researched, observer/observed, and healthy/ill dichotomy between us was dismantled as I was overcome physically with tears before her when faced with her approaching death.

The most profound of these inversions came the night we coauthored her wishes, side by side in her hospital bed, my laptop balanced on my legs. Again, in one of the most activist experiences of literacy in my life, I was overcome by the honesty of the composing act: our writing was a mutual acknowledgment, a pact of sorts between us, that she was reaching the last days of her life. I was mourning my friend beside me while we wrote together, choosing the best words to provide comfort and direction for those she loved. But I was equally overcome by the reach and power of our text: as the words appeared on my computer screen, Sue seemed to gain a sort of control over her own decline; she began to claim her own terms. There was some strange comfort in this nearness to death. It felt to me like a kind of wrangling, and I could sense her relief and joy as the text took shape. I wept beside her when the document was complete, full of this strange wonder and yet also steeped in my own anticipatory grief. In an effort to comfort me, Sue put her arm around me and whispered, "I don't want to die, Jess." And then: "It doesn't hurt." The first words came out as an assurance but one stripped of any desperation or anger: not wanting to die was merely her way of telling me that her psychology was essentially in check. She was not driving her own death forward out of extraordinary frustration, depression, or a desire to escape her own suffering. She wanted to live, just as I did. We were the same in this way. But what she communicated next—*it doesn't hurt*—was a second appeal to our bodily contact. Was I mourning her physical pain? Was I mourning her suffering? Was I frightened for her? Addressing my own capacity to experience bodily pain, she pulled us together into a shared experiential space: *it doesn't hurt*. Of course, Sue could not undo or prevent my loss, or the loss many others—especially her children—would endure upon her death. But she could traverse what seemed at the moment to be the vast physical space between us—bodies in illness and health—by speaking directly to my own bodily experience of being essentially pain-free. We were suddenly the same in this way—not physically in pain—and that brought me comfort. I could understand what she was feeling by feeling my own body. Van Manen argues that touch serves the "need of finding a *livable relation*" to the body for the seriously ill (7). I would add here that, in our inversion, Sue led me back to my own body as the locus for a "livable relation" to her embodied experience in that moment. By assuring me she did not want to die, she also communicated that the feeling of being alive—another livable relation—was still preferable to her (as it was to me in my body) despite her physical state, which, again, did not hurt.

Similar points of shared bodily experience would serve this rhetorical bridging function on multiple occasions as Sue's illness progressed, even when these same points of bodily relation ultimately served to illuminate what had become our very different bodily states. Our experience of athleticism became a site of physical communication for us. We used this to understand what we could, and this understanding happened in exchange, a kind of partnership in coming to terms. I return to a moment: the occasion toward the end of her life when Sue insisted that we go for a walk after directing my attention to her legs: "'I have to move, Jess. Look at my legs. They are so skinny, wasting away. Let's go'" (Restaino, "Reflection: Walk to Lake"). Physical activity was a salve to us both, a solution to problems of the body and even the mind. I wrote later a description of this walk:

> We walked—as you wanted—all the way to the lake, one mile there, you told me. Slow but steady. And our destination, as you chose for us: a gazebo on the edge of a small beach, staring out onto the water. My breath caught when you hesitated—one step up, falter, wait, rock, second step up. And then we sat.

I understood implicitly the problem/solution link between Sue's legs ("so skinny, wasting away") and the impulse to exercise ("I have to move, Jess"). I also understood Sue's impulse to record the mileage for our walk, as distance was a measure of her stamina, that she could in fact "move" there and back again. Of course, destabilizing my own body—*my breath caught when you hesitated*—was my observation of her physical difficulty, that it was in fact hard to walk and even harder to go two steps up. This naturally was both a point of connection and disconnection, as I understood Sue's body as inherently strong and capable and—as an athlete myself—tend in general to hold expectations for my own bodily performance: my body can run x miles. This is undoubtedly a position steeped in privileged assumptions, as Jay Dolmage reminds us: "The term *normate* designates the subject position of the supposedly (or temporarily) able-bodied individual" (23). Drawing on Aristotle, Dolmage points at our contemporary "normative mandate . . . the systematic self- and other-surveillance and bodily discipline of normative processes" (23). In a sense, Sue and I coexisted in such an orientation to our respective bodies. It is fair, I believe, to say that for both of us the coming-to-terms with what she *was not able* to do was indeed a kind of loss, a reason for mourning. Surely this sadness was steeped in the expectations we each held for bodily normativity but also—unique to terminal illness—in the underlying awareness that she was not moving into a "new normal" but rather what would be a continual decline.

Against the backdrop of Sue's shifting abilities, we also shared the expectation that movement is fundamentally healing, a notion inevitably undone by terminal illness that, again, incrementally scales back what is possible for the body. In the case of our walk to the lake it was mostly just exhausting for her, "then we sat." The futility of exercise to improve what was ultimately her failing liver, and the extent to which her failing liver further made exercise itself increasingly impossible, shook the fundamental understanding and respective embodied experiences we held between us. Still, in desperation we each tried to cling to the idea for as long as we could. She wrote me one day in July, about a month and a half before her death, of her frustration: "It sounds to me like the hour or so I'm exercising I'm putting myself in danger of bleeding but long term is a benefit" (Maute, "Re: I Love You"). Entwined painfully here—for me certainly still as I read and write now alone—is the association of exercise with time, with guaranteed time. Exercise, as Sue casts it, "long term is a benefit." I am reminded again of Corder's hopeful claim about time: "Since we don't have time, we must rescue time by putting it into our discourses and holding it there" ("Argument as Emergence" 31). Indeed, contemporary disability studies scholarship asks us to think about "crip time," this notion of "'satisfaction in statis,'" which terminal illness at once uniquely offers (a good month? a good week? a good day?) and yet ultimately denies (Walters 159). In our exchange, it is the body that might "rescue" itself from its own temporal decline: exercise functions here to extend time, "long term," even as the body presents concurrently with other threats, "danger of bleeding." The rhetorical, intellectual, even spiritual challenge embedded here is to rethink rescue altogether, as it is neither time nor the body that can be saved. Once again, I return to Halberstam's feminist project "that fails to save others or to replicate itself, a feminism that finds purpose in its own failure" (128). How does rhetoric function to usher in such feminist failure? What is the role of the body—the dying body *and* the body of data before us—in a rhetorical exchange grounded in what cannot be realized, accomplished, fully understood, fixed, or resolved?

I (researcher) need to feel that I can't understand your (participant) experience.

While bodily contact has an unmatched capacity to pull us rhetorically together into intimate understanding, equally important and very near is its opposite capacity: to engage us experientially, in body, with our own inability to understand. This is often a two-step process that in fact begins with similarity: we first have a "livable relation" that allows us to recognize the incomprehensibility of the *other* body. Disconnection is delivered just steps beyond connection, but we must be willing to travel to what is often the uncomfortable, disturbing edge in order to touch (literally and figuratively) our own limits to understanding. Dolmage warns us of the predictable, narrowing rhetorics around discoveries of difference: "Normativity also works through exnomination: an elaborate taxonomy of abnormality is created and applied. Ability is anchored and erected through the labeling of disability" (29). Here though too, for

Dolmage, is potential, as "disability is so naturally and habitually associated with negativity" that any move to question ("the pause, reflection, and reconsideration") stands to open "critical and creative opportunities" (286).[5] Of course, touch always has the capacity for disconnection, for a widening or illustration of vast negativity or "not me," because it always has the capacity for violence.[6] But Dolmage, I would argue, in his assertion about our tendency toward "exnomination" as a move to define disability, pushes here toward something more hopeful: an invention, an opportunity to reach new rhetorical ground, new identities, new ways of understanding if we pause and examine critically these levers toward negative "naming."

I thus move into this examination of "I can't understand" with great and sweeping hesitancy, well aware of the limits of my own writing and of the empowered position I hold in the body that has, essentially, *lived to tell* some aspects of another's story. Indeed, terminal illness draws the ultimate line in light of Dolmage's "exnomination." The markers of "living" and "dying" become ever more pronounced until the negative is brought into relief with seeming simplicity: to exist or not, to breathe or not, to be here or to be gone for good. However, even these markers are misleading, a claim I think Dolmage's work supports. My challenge then is to illustrate the productivity, the generative quality of what I could not—and still can't—understand of Sue's experience, while neither slipping into a sort of "negative habitus" nor taking refuge in the postmodern claim that "all language is disabled," which, as Dolmage warns, "camouflages oppression" (287). Terminal illness is an oppressive force all its own, one that disempowers not only the body it inhabits but also the surrounding healthy bodies that must contend with their failed capacity to revise the course of disease, undoubtedly failures of "rescue," to draw again on Halberstam. Terminal illness thus orchestrates perhaps the most extreme version of Monica Clarke's claim "'I am outside myself'" (qtd. in Van Manen 21). We might think of this outsider status as an embodied dislocation from one's sense of potency: literally none of us, healthy or ill, can act in a way that will alter the outcome. While Clarke's experience reorients her to her daughter's agency, terminal illness is unique instead for its total leveling of agency: no one can go back, undo, stop the progression into total loss.

This progression widens as it advances, pushing bodies and minds toward perhaps that very longing Corder laments, "the desire to hold some things from oblivion" ("Argument as Emergence" 260). This longing is a fraught and in some ways fruitless one, as Corder again reminds us, "I know that in trying to hold things, I too will vanish. I had hoped to be real, but I am only a vacancy in the air" (260). For my purposes, I want to suggest that this desire rests on the threshold of connection and disconnection, a bodily point of contact that renders us alternatingly familiar and alien.[7] For Sue and me, opportunities to contend with our widening differences were numerous and necessary. One of the most poignant was her swollen abdomen, a symptom of her failing liver, which gave her the shape of full-term pregnancy while, combined with other visual markers of her illness, leaving no uncertainty about her status as ill (and thus not pregnant). And yet this pregnant shape and indeed the lived experience of having a distended abdomen was one we shared, both of us having had the experience of maternity. And so it entered into our language first as a reference point, a commonality, even as her abdomen would ultimately be a marker of our great physical divide.

The movement of this phenomenon—the distended abdomen—from binding to distancing serves as a uniquely physical rhetoric occasioned by intimacy and care in our *dynamis*. In a recorded interview about four months before her death, Sue and I discussed her relationship to her body particularly given that she had now become physically "marked" by her disease. She begins by disowning this version of her body, or at least expressing a desire for separateness, though ultimately she recognizes her unique losses:

> I'm more detached only because I don't think it defines me, except when it comes to what I love to do best. I love to use my body physically, running and sports, what it gives me the ability to do. But from that perspective I'm frustrated and I feel very connected. (Maute, personal interview, 2 May 2014)

From here she expresses hope for a recovery of her strength, for a return to sport, and outlines plans for how she might resume physical activity—that thing to which she is "very connected"—while still hindered by her swollen abdomen. Ultimately Sue bridges two of our shared physical experiences—sport and maternity—in order to also talk about something entirely foreign to me, her audience, which is the fact that her abdomen is swollen not by pregnancy but by liver failure:

> I want to get a support belt . . . because the stomach muscles are weak, just like when you're pregnant. I just got a single band that sits kind of below that like shelf [*laugh*]. Just so I can see if I have that supported if that makes walking . . . if that helps it . . . and then go from there. But

117

when I get my energy back, I sort of feel better, now I'm just trying
to find ways of making what I want to have happen happen . . . like
trying to get out there and play tennis again, hockey. I thought about
hockey this morning . . . I thought, I'm getting there, like I can feel it.

In many ways, all of them painful to me as I sit here reading words that
are hers and still as dear to me as ever, Sue illustrates Corder's "desire to
hold some things from oblivion," at least in terms of her own embodied
experience. The hope for a return to the physical activity that defines
her, "what I love to do best," is a yearning for self, that version of herself
she knows and can recognize. Instead she exists (and resists) personally
in Dolmage's "exnomination," that space in which disability comes into
relief by negation, what I am not or cannot do, except, of course, the
looming identification for Sue is *with* disability even as she resists. Her
response is thus at once twofold and contradictory: to "detach" and yet
to link the two of us—we are physically alike across the chasm of her
current illness—in order to trace a path back to the body she knows,
"what it gives me the ability to do." I, too, can imagine returning to
a familiar, active body following the distortion and discomfort of an
extended belly, and Sue signals this to me: "The stomach muscles are
weak, just like when you're pregnant." I also resonate physically with
her claim that she can "feel" the sport we both love and through which
our friendship had initially flourished.

On the surface of our dialogue is for me the painful sense that Sue is,
just as Corder admits, fruitlessly reaching: "I know that in trying to hold
things, I too will vanish." Her problem-solving, her likening of our physical experiences, all stand to highlight the growing difference between us
while casting her as tangled in denial. But I would argue that this would
be a simplified reading, and one that fails to make room for what would
come next, which would be the more radical acknowledgment—again
through our bodies—of her dying. Instead, in pulling us rhetorically
together, Sue makes "real" for me her desires by identifying our bodies as
initially similar but hers, ultimately, as possibly changed forever. In our
recorded interview on the subject, I refer to what seems like an experience of "two" versions of her body. She responds, referring again to her
abdomen: "You can't bring it back . . . maybe one day this will go down,
but I'm not waiting around" (Maute, personal interview, 2 May 2014).
Entering into our dialogue now is the possibility that, in fact, her belly
might not ever return to "normal," and so her efforts to problem-solve
(a support belt, for example) are geared toward accommodating what

might be a permanent bodily state. She clings to a desire to still *do* the things through which she finds her identity, but she is willing to alter the method in order to "hold some things from oblivion." While she continues to indicate hope for change—"I'm getting there, like I can feel it"—she also problem-solves in the "now," a moment in which her body is not the one she recognizes.

This move, I would argue, functions as a key transitional point for coming to terms together about the fact not only of Sue's new or permanently changed body but also of its demise. This shift is ushered in first by her efforts at problem-solving: indeed, her urgency to restore certain activities simultaneously highlights those which are utterly impossible. A plastic tube designed to drain the excess fluid produced by a poorly functioning liver created a permanent wound where the tube exited her belly. This tube, which had on its end a small plastic nozzle, typically lay coiled on her belly when not in use, taped to her beneath sterile gauze. Such an apparatus is sadly familiar territory in the world of palliative care and terminal cancer. The fact of this tube was a source of both relief and permanent damage: for as long as her liver failed to do its full work, she would need the drain. And the drain, by its very nature and function, created a wound that could not heal. Instead her skin scabbed around the plastic, longing to heal a gap the body could not afford to close. Noting in our recorded conversation that she "can't go in the water" despite plans to visit the beach in the coming summer, Sue addresses with her characteristic humor what was my ensuing confusion about why she could not swim:

> The problem is the hole [*laughing*]. When I come out I'll be like . . . like the kids' diapers! So, you know, just running through that in my head. What do I normally do down there and what am I not going to be able to do when I'm down there? (Maute, personal interview, 2 May 2014)

At issue here is of course is the disruption of "normal" and the extent to which this wound, its apparatus, demands a reconfiguration of possibility, and maybe with no resolution or end date in livable sight.

Despite her impulse toward humor, in fact there was nothing funny about Sue's distended belly, the trapped fluid it housed, or the drain designed to relieve the ensuing pressure. There was instead extraordinary pain and vulnerability that found its way between us, into our dialogue, given our mutual acknowledgement of her growing abdomen. The physical pain inflicted by the stretching and weight of her belly occasioned

Sue's very first confession to me of her own uncertainty, lying on her side in the recliner in her family room one winter day, "Jess, I don't know if things are going to be okay." My response was, "I know you don't," so clear was the immediate reality at the time: the fluid buildup was a sign of major organ failure and the physical symptoms it caused, the pain and pressure, unbearable to imagine long-term. That day I had bought her some big T-shirts that could stretch to fit her belly, and these too, with their cheap material and oversized quality, seemed only to further illustrate the futility of the situation. This was still an early, very private admission between us at the start of what would be several months of continued suffering, hope, and struggle; but it was made possible by a physical reality neither of us could deny.

Sue's belly and the way it moved her into intimate talk also occasioned my own acknowledgment and coming to terms with her physical decline. My "I know you don't" was also "and neither do I," though that last admission I kept to myself. Indeed, I did not need to speak it, so entrenched in my acknowledgment of her uncertainty was my own. And this too was born of the physical reality between us: in fact I had cleaned her un-healing wound myself, coiled the tube neatly to her, covered it all with sterile gauze while being careful to protect her weakened immune system and open wound from my own skin, my hands in rubber gloves, all material handled methodically to avoid contamination by the everyday germs on the tips of my fingers. Such physical helping, and the rhetorical transaction it occasions, is extraordinarily complex and intimate. As I cared for Sue's wound, I was no doubt in contact with *not me*, to draw on Dolmage's notion of exnomination, so poignant was the urgency of this foreign wound as a sign of our difference. But I was simultaneously, in this very act, also deeply, rhetorically, and physically drawn into fuller understanding of her illness, her bodily frailty, her need for assistance in ways that opened my capacity for making meaning of her coming death. This meaning making did not exist merely in the private confines of my own mind. It would be essential to fostering my status as her audience, her listener, making possible my response "I know you don't," thus honoring her admission of uncertainty and need to be recognized as potentially dying. Of course I knew. I had cleaned her wound, coiled the tube, emptied the accumulating bags of excess fluid—each a symbol of all her liver could not manage—myself, by hand.

Shannon Walters describes a radical moment of transactional physical care between disability rights activist Harriet McBride Johnson and her debate opponent the controversial bioethicist Peter Singer, known for his support of infanticide in the case of severely disabled infants. Johnson and Singer had attended a university-hosted dinner following their public debate; Johnson ultimately asked Singer for needed assistance as he sat beside her at the dinner table. Walters describes this moment between two otherwise-rivals as "based in an interconnectedness and lived reality . . . a response that changes based on the needs of the situation" (163). Walters goes on to more fully explain the rhetorical capacity of touch in transgressing or communicating the lines drawn by disability:

> If touch is truly a *dynamis*, a potential for grasping meaning in new ways, then what must we hold on to and let go of to fully realize touch as a rhetorical and ethical art? . . . Touch also invites us to more comprehensively let go of the idealized image of an independent, nondisabled, singular rhetor and to embrace the possibilities of new configurations among communicators, speaking and nonspeaking, and multiple audiences across ranges of ability and disability. (199)

Terminal breast cancer answers Walters's question first and foremost with an eager dismissal of "pink warrior" narratives. Returning to Jackie Rhodes's exploration of subjectivity in the digital text "Rhizomes," I am reminded of what Rhodes describes as the danger of "narrative inclusion," that move to "contain difference in order to make it legible, identifiable, and thus acceptable to a normative readership." Juxtaposed with Dolmage's treatment of exonomination, we find new pathways to recognize and authorize difference as generative: indeed our identities must not behave. As I discussed earlier in the book, "pink warriors" in the popular Western narrative around breast cancer take on mythic qualities; these qualities are laced with our fantasies of inhuman toughness, fight, a capacity for endurance and suffering that exceeds what any "normal" person could manage. In Sue's resistance to the traditional pink warrior narrative—*I don't want the word "battle" used at any point during services for me. Nothing like "her courageous fight" or some bullshit*—she misbehaves as a terminal cancer patient character in a well-worn narrative, the one that renders her difference "acceptable to a normative readership" (Maute, "What I Want"). She refuses her status as a hero of epic proportions, that rare, inspiring superhuman whose capacity exceeds that of the rest of us, and thus she also refuses to affirm that the rest of us are safely distanced from the very battle only a true hero can fight.

Touch, then, to answer part of Walters's question, invites us to *let go* of notions of the superhuman, the ever-so-different, by putting us in contact with each other's physical vulnerability, need for care, indeed our fragile beings. This fragility can be communicated—with attunement and respect—in ways that not only illuminate difference (that is, I understand, in touching your body, what my own body is not) but also put us in contact with our own physical vulnerabilities, the uncertain status of our bodies at any moment in time. Touch can usher in our comprehension of that which is still outside the confines of our own physical walls but, by the very nature of shared materiality, indicates a frailty that is still also possible to us. To return again to Jessica Benjamin's work on the repair of collective trauma, such embodied contact allows for us to hold between us the intersubjective tension "I could never imagine/I could imagine" ("Discarded and the Dignified" 3). Benjamin describes this as "accepting badness" in the work of healing collective trauma specific to war, political violence, and other civil rights violations where seemingly unthinkable violation has been inflicted by opposing forces (3). Repair requires that such atrocities become somehow "imaginable," that the otherwise incomprehensible becomes comprehensible, possible, particularly in the absence of retaliation by the victim.

Thus terminal breast cancer—or at least the *dynamis* I shared with Sue—answers the other part of Walters's question, "what must we hold on to," with an assertion of Benjamin's "badness": our capacity for weakness, for sickness, for failure. We are in contact with that which we otherwise cannot imagine. Bodies—bodies in illness, bodies of data, bodies in contact—make possible rhetorical transactions that get us nearer to, put us in touch with, make us imagine *badness*. To the extent that my use of the word "badness" here might be misconstrued as a labeling of disability itself as "bad," I call instead for a deeper significance. In our own "badness" we might find our fuller potential, even if that potential remains outside of our current lived experience. As I think both Dolmage's and Walters's work makes clear, these intersections and reimaginings are generative. For Walters, moments of rhetorical touch such as those shared by Johnson and Singer are kairotic, "a locus of bodies and materials in contact and movement and often a space in which 'warps' or non-normative locations are productive" (157). For Benjamin, this is best encapsulated in the assertion, which I explored earlier in the book, "'I wanted to sleep in the sweat of the woman who forgave my brother'" ("Discarded" 9). Again, here Benjamin describes a scene from the documentary film *One Day after Peace*, in which a grieving mother seeks to forgive the man who killed her daughter randomly in the midst of a militia attack in South Africa. The sentiment belongs to the killer's sister and, for Benjamin, represents a "visceral metaphor of skin and sweat" that "exemplif[ies] the overcoming of bodily separation on which we found our dissociation from the other's pain" (9). Indeed, this notion of "overcoming" is of course partial: "the sweat" is merely "'of the woman'" and decidedly not the woman herself, but what the physical act renders is desire, one that cannot be satisfied by words alone. And this desire indicates an openness to *badness*: I *could* imagine.

Imperfect as our desires and imaginings are, they are often the best we can do and they are—indeed—rhetorical, by which I mean that they are efforts to bring ourselves and others *closer* into understanding across difference. Our rhetorical moves are perhaps never complete, but by their very enactment and reenactment, we render and expose our desires. In his essay "From Rhetoric to Grace," Corder casts it thus:

> The paradigm dramatically presented by rhetoric puts us always in process. The language we use is never enough, but we get to return, if we will, and say more. The paradigm shows us grace. This grace is always being sought, always available, never being fully found because our limits will not let us say or show everything. We cannot put our limitations or sins behind us: we go forward in their presence, in the presence of such lies, deceits, failures, and small successes as may belong to us, trying to make something of what we have done and what we are. . . . Grace works in humans when they acknowledge the limitations of their closed speech and turn again in openness to a new invention. (27)

I quote Corder at length here because I believe he offers us useful access to Benjamin's "I could never imagine/I could imagine." To the extent that we might willingly return to "say more" or to *hear* or *touch* more, we expand what is possible in terms of what we both can and cannot understand. The latter, too, is a rhetorical transaction: in engaging with the limits of what I can experience, I illuminate our differences, what exceeds my grasp. In terms of thinking about the research collaboration and its capacity for knowledge making, questions become these: How might we redefine our roles and expectations in terms of pursuing, as a goal, contact with our limits to comprehension? What methods might we put in place for bringing us closer to such an objective? Of course my work here offers only one configuration among unique circumstances, and yet an overarching message might be that we make space for intimate rhetorical contact, for feeling the edges of what we can recognize and what we can't, and that we risk such intimacy and care in the research relationship and in how we handle the data generated between and among us.

I (participant) need you (researcher) to take care of my body so I (as represented by the body) am safe and valued.

I would argue that the move into openness, to "badness," or to what we might think of as the width of Benjamin's "I could never imagine/I could imagine" makes possible through care and compassion fuller, deeper use of our data. The embodied rhetorics occasioned by terminal illness introduce data that we might think of as challenging, grotesque, indeed the physical manifestation of badness. This is the body in its decline, with all of its needs for care, rendered ultimately intolerable or potentially repulsive. Terminal illness models or occasions a particular way of doing our work.[8] What are the benefits to the work produced, to the researcher who is made and remade in the work, to the writing as it is rendered? I propose that we think of all data—any data—as presenting a range of possibilities that might challenge our capacity for badness, stretch our limits beyond what we believe we "could never imagine."

This proposal ushers in a unique set of challenges. How do we support (perhaps even encourage) the emergence of such data in the research process? What is the role of the researcher-writer in responding to—or indicating an acceptance of—"bad" data? In other words, how do we indicate to our research participants that there is, indeed, *no* bad data, that all data—however painful, grotesque, or frightening—have a place in our collaborative understanding of how words work between us to create meaning, texts, and valued knowledge? I want to offer a particularly painful story in relation to Sue's vulnerability to internal bleeding, a topic with which I opened the chapter. My goal in sharing this story, certainly a frightening event and now a haunting memory, is that we might imagine the generative, creative, and rhetorical quality of "bad data." I hope, too, that I am able to tell this story with tremendous care and respect for my friend.

Sue was in and out of the hospital with depressing regularity in the last two months of her life. And so I return again to a now-familiar scene: an internal bleed, her esophagus. She texted me early in the morning—"Heading to hospital throwing up blood in significant quantities . . ." ("Re: Heading to hospital")—and, following an emergency procedure by a gastroenterologist to secure the ruptures with bands, we sat together in her hospital room awaiting the next step in the repair process, a blood transfusion. She had lost much blood; she needed three pints to get to safe levels. Adding to the uncertainty of the situation, the hospital did not have an available bed on the oncology floor; this meant Sue was with nurses who did not work regularly with cancer patients. To the uninitiated, this might not seem like much of a big deal; but to those in the taxing throes of terminal cancer, oncology-focused nurses are unflinching, essential navigators of the otherwise foreign terrain of chemo ports, abdominal drains, and certainly the trauma of internal bleeds. As we waited for what was next, we held this tension, this awareness that we were not quite in the right place, knowingly between us.

Well before the arrival of the life-giving bags of blood for transfusion and while the two of us sat quietly alone together, Sue suddenly began to vomit much of the blood she had inadvertently swallowed during the earlier bleed. We had no idea at the time what the reason was for this second round of terrible retching, nor could either of us do more than respond in the moment to the situation at hand. We each tried with some futility to take care of the other: me, holding a plastic bin before her and talking softly about how it was all going to be okay (*was it!? "okay"!?*); her, trying delicately to wipe her mouth in between heaves and narrating to me softly. It was indeed awful. It was indeed a living nightmare. Both of us were aware that the nurses I had yelled for had arrived in the doorway, a staring pair, and ultimately disappeared together, muttering some excuse about looking for a doctor as they ran away. There was a terrible quiet following this episode. I had placed the plastic bin to the side, saving it for inspection by the doctor, whenever that doctor might arrive. Only a few minutes following the event, a visitor arrived for Sue, entering unknowingly into the thickness of the privately shared trauma between us, slicing with distanced niceties the stunned quiet that hung in our air, a yet-unmet need to look at each other and ask, *What just happened here?*

I found myself mourning the fact of this episode in the days that followed. Beyond the obvious pain of the event itself, there was something extraordinary about Sue's gentle efforts to communicate with me in its midst. I wrote reflectively in hopes of capturing my perception of both her suffering and her attempts at care and composure:

> You know how it went, that you were so ill, there was a lot of dark, clotted blood, and even the nurses were scared and backed away, left us—actually—to *both* go find a doc. I did not want to leave, did not want to run. You cried, said "Jess I don't like feeling like this . . ." and yet somehow you even tried to be funny or make a comment, with

your attitude still in check, while you retched over the plastic bin I
held in front of you.

I don't know how much of the rest of our time went that afternoon.
I think I left shortly after new visitors arrived . . . your sister, maybe,
your sister-in-law, all after the worst of it. That was just between
you and me, the awfulness. I felt like this was as it should have been.
(Restaino, "Reflection: Week of 7/7/14")

Mixed in here is my own impulse to return the spirit of choice and care:
indeed, I was not trapped, not a victim to this episode, not an unwilling
participant, "I did not want to leave, did not want to run." A new way
of knowing myself: I could not have anticipated my reaction to this and
other such wrenching events; but what I learned amid such experiences
was a desire to be present. I am not suggesting that I learned I could
easily tolerate or bear, as a friend or partner in this process, the "awfulness." But if given the opportunity, the choice, I would choose presence
and participation. I started, too, to feel as though our partnership, the
roots of which began in a far more formal reading and writing endeavor,
had emerged as inevitable, necessary, "as it should be." We became two
who shared the awfulness.

This, of course, did not mean we could or would experience any of it
in the same way. We remained bound together by a mutual desire for the
presence of the other, though perhaps from opposite sides of the same
room. I suppose, as I look back now, that I clung to her in some ways in
order to keep her, while she clung to me in hopes that I could acknowledge her need to let go. There was in either case a sense of sweeping loss
that we kept tightly between us. And indeed it was our "bad data," those
moments of deepest awfulness, of badness, that melted our respective,
perhaps conflicting needs into something of a shared mission. The day
following the incident, I arrived at the hospital shortly before Sue was
to be discharged. I return to a scene of my own written reflection:

When I came by on Friday, I knew I'd be the one to take you home
from the hospital. I don't know what you knew beforehand, I don't
know how you had talked through the plans to leave, or if you really
did . . . but I knew it'd be me. I walked into the room and you were
curled in the chair by the window. You looked so small. No lights
were on in the room, but there was a lot of sunlight. You seemed to
be trying to soak it in, even as you were so dry and worn looking. You
looked sick in the sunlight, your hair brittle and short to your head,
your neck and face thin.

I sat on the edge of the bed and we were instantly in a place together, an island of a kind, the one that I can't seem to fully describe
to anyone or fully share. You were sad and reflective, quiet, and I
knew you'd be worried about going home. We don't have to rush, I
thought. There's no rush. (Restaino, "Reflection: Week of 7/7/14")

The conversation that ensued was one of caretaking: Sue offering something of a soft apology for the ugly incident of the preceding day, me
insisting that—just as I had written—I had been where I wanted to be,
wouldn't have it any other way. Still, "'just as a friend, you know,'" she
checked on me. For my part I had begun to accept an inevitable quality
to our togetherness: this sentiment came to me without reluctance or
dread but rather a kind of intimate knowing, a personal acknowledgment
that I was with her—would be with her—for the whole of it and that the
"whole of it" would include suffering and loss. I would—as would others
in intimate relation with her—be on an island all my own eventually.
Indeed, as I look back now on our presentation at the Feminisms and
Rhetorics Conference in the fall of 2013, just a year into our efforts to
collect, describe, write, and talk our way through Sue's illness together,
I can see that I ultimately came to answer my own questions, "How far
have I surrendered? How much further will I go? These are questions
I ask while I wonder if answers—any answers—are even within reach"
(Restaino and Maute, "No Evidence" 16).[9]

In "Crash: What We Do When We Cannot Touch," Jessica Benjamin describes the phenomenon of relational impasse in the therapeutic
dyad in terms of a patient's description of the experience as a "crash."
We might think of rhetorical touch itself, particularly at its most challenging limits, as potentially a "crash" of sorts, indeed both a literal and
figurative coming into jarring, destabilizing contact. Benjamin quotes a
scene from the film *Crash* to make an argument for the essential value
of impasse and conflict: "'We don't touch. Maybe we have to crash into
each other because we have not been touching'" (377). Fundamental
here, for Benjamin, is the "move between withdrawal and connecting . . .
rupture and repair" (378). When rhetorical touch occasions such rupture
in our collaborations or interactions, drawing a physical boundary line
enabled by our bodies between what we can and cannot understand or
experience, we are left to come to rhetorical terms with each other; we
must reorient ourselves if we are to move forward in relationship.

While much compelling scholarship exists on agonistic rhetoric, I
put forth this seemingly overlapping notion of "crash" in the context

of rhetorical touch because I believe it makes possible consideration of—and care for—"bad" or grotesque data in ways that traditional thinking about the rhetorical agon simply does not.[10] There is a passivity, vulnerability, indeed a capacity for victimization ushered in by a crash: we crash not because we are fighting but because we are hurled together at speeds at which we each, respectively, lack control. The terminally ill body shares this pace, this experience of flying into or toward something certain to inflict damage. And the opportunity to crash—to come into such chaotic, destabilizing contact—opens for us the possibility of a kind of subversive knowledge making in the spirit of Halberstam's "radical passivity." Halberstam situates this project in Gayatri Chakravorty Spivak's "largely unanswered" call for "indeed any kind of intellectual who can learn how not to know the other, how not to sacrifice the other on behalf of his or her own sovereignty" (Spivak et al. 128).[11] Our *crashing into* each other as research collaborators opens us to, indeed invents between us, the "bad data" that can nourish a rhetorical undoing of self and other. Bad data—and only bad data—invite the opportunity to hold that which, in exceeding words, communicates extraordinary vulnerability and value, making possible, again to draw on Walters, "working at the edges of language" (199).

Halberstam offers Yoko Ono's work *Cut Piece* as a representation of the radical passivity at the heart of Spivak's imagined feminist intellectual, and, while I gave this example attention earlier in the book, I return here because the scene I described between Sue and me at the start of this chapter can at last be more fully understood in connection to Ono's performance piece. Again, in *Cut Piece*, Ono sits passively on stage while audience members are invited, one at a time, to come up and cut away pieces of her clothing, revealing her increasing nudity and ultimate bodily vulnerability. Halberstam describes Ono's positionality here as "commitment to the fragment of the whole over any fantasy of future wholeness" (138). Terminal illness demands an honoring of the fragmentary in the most extreme, extraordinary way: in fact "the whole" is coming apart. It will soon be no longer. The body itself is falling to pieces. The frightening episode shared between Sue and me enacts this very physical and conceptual fact. The body is not holding together, and thus any recognition of the body—*any* body—acknowledges its capacity to literally fall to pieces. This is as true for my body as it is—or was—for hers. This is also true for other, seemingly innocuous "bodies" of data, interview transcripts, for example, imbued with real voices or, as Mazzei uncovers in interrogating her own work, real and substantive silences.

What significance does Ono's performance assign to audience members, those doing the actual "cutting," and how might my role as researcher—or any of us who work with bad or grotesque data—be pivotal here? Indeed as researchers, whether acknowledged or not, we are always also cutters, taking apart not just our data and our research participants but also ourselves. In our cutting and even in our eventual, sometimes reassembling, we do meaningful damage and have an opportunity to feel something at once terrifying and inexplicable. The feminism for which Halberstam calls, again, "fails to save others or to replicate itself, a feminism that finds purpose in its own failure." This is about exposing our handiwork, its ultimate futility, and, I would argue, such exposure is double-sided: we are simultaneously limited in our capacity to understand and render the other, and ourselves. The harder we try, in fact, the greater damage we might do. How, as researcher-writers, might we contend with this danger? How might we do it justice and honor (recognize?) our capacity for harm? To what extent might such danger—and the risk-taking it invites—invent new kinds of knowledge, texts, and ways of doing research? How might our own *badness* remake us? Returning to Walters's opening reference, in what ways might Sullivan, Keller's very own "cutter," have exposed her subjective limits to knowing and doing as she worked to cut and assemble and, thus, ultimately touch the borders of Keller's disability?

Benjamin offers the perspective of the analyst amid the "crash" who "cannot avoid a subjective fear of reinflicting the wound and must deal with her own fear of causing terrible pain" ("Crash" 383). Such subjective fear, I would argue, might be shared by perhaps all researcher-writers, but certainly by those of us who work in spaces of pain, loss, and vulnerability. While this phenomenon is informed by work in disability rhetorics, I offer a necessary caveat to avoid sweeping generalization: the suggestion that those with disabilities are indeed in "terrible pain" as the link to Benjamin's analyst might suggest here is not a move I wish to make. As Eli Clare reminds us, "'In the moments when I become someone's supercrip or tragedy: all those lies become my second skin'" (qtd. in Walters 151).[12] As Clare's language suggests, any move to "own"—"when I become someone's"—can be oppressive and colonizing. Both the radical passivity that Ono's work enacts and the sort of feminism Halberstam claims resist owning, saving, or replicating. Instead the radical feminist move here is toward existence with our own unique fragmentation, loss, and failure. Terminal illness removes traditional notions of triumph, cure, and—certainly in the case of breast cancer, this is most profound—bodily wholeness.

But how do I make any sense of me, scissors in hand? How do I function as Sue's cutter and her collaborator all at once? What do I fear and what damage have I done, particularly in this chapter where I have rendered her so ill, so vulnerable in body? Indeed, I write terrified. And this fear stretches across my text as itself a vulnerable body, into my love for my friend and my desire not to hurt her, to misrepresent her, to objectify her pain or her suffering, to my sense of myself as an imperfect, fragmentary author, and on through my own living body as, in taking physical care of her body, I have also touched my own capacity for illness. Surprisingly, Benjamin's prediction for the outcome of such fear amid a "crash" in the therapeutic dyad is a hopeful, if radical, one. She describes the analyst who "actually is destroyed and able to recover from it, falling apart and coming back together as a usable object" ("Crash" 383). If I imagine the researcher-writer role in these terms, I face some serious questions: Have I fallen apart? And if so, what does it mean to come back together? How have I changed? How fragmentary do I remain? And if I am indeed a kind of "usable object," what is my use amid all these glued-together pieces?

These questions necessitate yet another reconsideration of Corder's fruitless wish, "I had hoped to be real, but I am only a vacancy in the air." It's hard to fully discern what Corder's "real" might look like, though to some extent his writing suggests a yearning for a "whole" subject, one that remains unchanged by (or despite) its interactions with others.[13] I also resist this notion of being a "vacancy," which suggests one—in either body or text or certainly both—might just become empty space entirely, in fact nothing to retain or hold onto. In facing her own mortality, Sue inevitably explored similarly dark corners and yet embraced the uncertainty that seems out of Corder's reach here. In one of our most important recorded conversations, she reflected on the possibility of her death, particularly when her liver had first started to fail earlier that winter. I quote her at length here:

> Well I just feel like I'm going to be okay. And I don't know why I feel this. I don't know if it's just me trying to kid myself or if I'm avoiding . . . I can't get a handle on it. Like [counselor] back in December when things were really bad . . . after I had all that news. And she

said "How's this all making you feel?" and I still said, "I don't know why but I still feel like I'm going to be okay." Like even in the throes of how bad it was . . . I mean, it was bad and I was scared and I was like freaking out . . . like, *oh my God*, "forever" . . . that concept's hard to grasp: gone forever? . . . But at the same time I just have this overwhelming feeling that I'm going to be okay. And I don't know what that means. I don't know if that means like after I die or that I'm going to live another twenty years. (Personal interview, 2 May 2014)

From the time of this interview, Sue would live another four months. But it does not quite matter, at least not in the term she recasts here: "be okay." This idea of being okay is one she pushes beyond any notion of a cure, of recovery, of becoming in a sense "whole" again, or in terms of countable years. It did not matter that she'd live merely months, a stretch of weeks, rather than another full year, let alone twenty. She identifies no conditions for being okay. In redefining this colloquialism against the expectations we typically hold for illness and health, she also invites me, as her collaborator, to rethink my role too, how I have behaved and how I might make sense of my status. What if what I now "am" is merely someone who has gotten *closer* to that which I could not fully understand? Perhaps I am someone who has lost irreparably and who writes incompletely now. And maybe in my assembling of words, my efforts to render her and also us, I have exposed my weaknesses, my vulnerability, made my very own exnominating move, to draw on Dolmage: I have cut openings all around these pages, revealing what I am not and what I can't do. Into this text I have surrendered all of it.

While I will not—and how could I?—argue for a singular method for writing and research that might embody the lessons of mutual failing embedded here, I do want to suggest that my collaboration with Sue might model one way of engaging in work that destroys us for a good cause. In fact we ought to be destroyed, over and over again, by all that we can't understand, and that includes the pain inflicted by those other forces that tower like terminal illness: racism, sexism, misogyny, homophobia, and ableism, to name just a few. This means that, as researchers and as writers, we occasion and allow for our own falling to pieces on the faith that indeed we may come back together again, though changed, our own holes now gaping in ways we had not known possible. Perhaps we had no idea there were holes in our pages to begin with, that our data hid from us their grotesqueness, that our participants said more in silence, as Lisa Mazzei and Cheryl Glenn surely have both argued, than we could ever understand. How might we render our writerly subjectivity in ways that sur*render* its palatability or wholeness? Psychoanalytic theorist Michael Eigen casts it as a faith in "murder": "I think this faith has in it a love of life. It opens heartwide and cannot stop opening. It is a faith that is stronger than murder, that makes murder fruitful" (738). How do we hold between us, as scholars, research collaborators, coauthors, a relationship to language that hinges innovation to our own failure, our exposed falling-to-pieces in our work? In the following chapter I will respond with a radical argument for love.

BLOODWORK
(A TEXT MESSAGE)

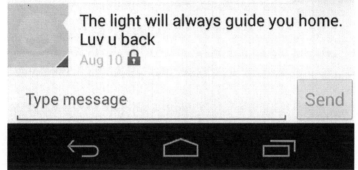

Rode the light all the way home. ;) I love you, my friend. xo

🔒 Aug 10

The light will always guide you home. Luv u back

Aug 10 🔒

Type message   Send

Sue and I imagine the cosmic. *Restaino and Maute, text message correspondence, 10 Aug. 2014.*

IN SITU
LOVE AS FRAME

As O'Reilly puts it, "It is love, after all . . . that keeps the moral world with its irreconcilable oppositions from flying apart like a stunned asteroid." Rhetoric can assist us in channeling that moral force in magical, deliberate, and deeply satisfying ways. (Ervin, "Love" 329)

Consider my ongoing struggle with how to represent Jim Corder in this essay—as "Jim," the man, or as "Corder," the academic. It's a ridiculous distinction, really, for Jim-the-man *was* Jim-the-academic. The fact that I find it so difficult to integrate the two demonstrates the limitations of an academic discourse incapable of accommodating even *coherent* multiple narratives, roles, and identities. (329)

These two quotations are excerpts from Elizabeth Ervin's "Love Composes Us (in Memory of Jim Corder)," which, as the title suggests, memorializes Jim Corder following his death in 1998. Ervin had been a graduate student of Corder's and admits that in those early days,

I didn't have the confidence to embrace Jim's slow, patient, meditative ways; I aspired to mainstream accomplishments earned in the most mainstream (and preferably expeditious) fashion, which included "mastery" of the typical forms of academic argument that I. A. Richards has described as a "battle of words." (323)

But writing years later, remembering Jim and in particular his essay "Argument as Emergence, Rhetoric as Love," Ervin admits, "But like many of my colleagues, I've lost my taste for blood over the years" (323). Even still, it's hard to write about love and feel serious. "And why is that?" Ervin muses. "Is it because love itself has been Oprahfied beyond recovery?" (322). Is it because, she wonders, the nature and scope and culture of our professional lives "seem inhospitable to loving behavior" (322)? "There appears," Ervin notes with sadness, "no principled means of yielding to others without being coopted or losing face" (322).

In this chapter I gather together into one space the spirits whose magic has been pushing these pages forward all along and advance an argument for love. Both magic and love are multiply defined and in all counts can embarrass even as they persuade us. Sue and I used to joke, when her illness was finally so visible that strangers on the street would either stare at or bless her (sometimes both), that she had become somehow "cosmic": this is our "ride the light" reference in the opening "Bloodwork" for this chapter. She had on one occasion been sitting on a bench outside the hospital, waiting for me to bring the car around to take her home, and a man sitting beside her, someone she had never met, read her physical frailty and baldness and whispered to her blessings toward her "fight" and her "strength." She got into my car afterward, told me the story quickly, and joked that she imparted on him the other-worldly wisdom "ride the light" as a kind of parting gift, a playful embodiment of his reading her as larger or perhaps more celestial than in fact she felt herself to be. Love is sometimes shamefully big like that too: like a kind of magic, bigger and more powerful than we can fully imagine in any rational way.

Sue indeed played with, resisted, and was darkly entertained by her experiences of being read as transcendent or inspirational; this play became part of our relationship, our ongoing talk.[1] At the same time, if (and when) we were being totally honest, I'd also say we were unified, if secretive, believers in the magic that swirled around Sue's experience of dying. Indeed, when we quipped in a text message—*rode the light/the light will always guide you home*—we were also quietly buoyed, transfixed perhaps, our sights set on something that felt big enough to believe in (while we tried fiercely to get the irony). I suppose I should accuse myself here of unfairly speaking for my friend on this issue of belief; I suppose I should attest only to my own position, claim these vulnerabilities entirely, as I write alone now of course. But then I remember how, that night when we coauthored her final wishes, she made me help her to the hospital room window so she could see the moon. It was glorious: full and silver and seeming to sit right on the rooftops. She wanted me to text her when I got home—it was after midnight—so she knew I was safe and sound: "rode the light all the way home," I assured her. And maybe indeed I did. Magic, spirits, some sort of acquiescence to the irrational, if you will: this project represents my own "yielding," to draw on Ervin. I have been broken and confounded and yet also uplifted over the years of this work. I experienced Sue's death as an extraordinary loss. It was not merely a source of great sadness but a reconfiguring of belief. Coming to know her as dying was a long-term, slow, painful disintegration of a faulty (and unfair) belief in her as superhuman or at least unbreakable. I could throw childish temper tantrums but to no avail. But again in "falling apart" there is, as Jessica Benjamin tells us, possibility: "coming back together as a usable object" ("Crash" 383). And though I work now to determine anew my use value, I find myself routinely awash in gratitude, the recipient of some unasked-for gift of reseeing and rethinking.[2]

I do know my status is still of believer—still of writer, researcher, teacher, collaborator, friend—but altered. And the first full step forward I want to take, reconstructed and faulty as I am, is one that acknowledges the irrational rhetorics of love and magic, to draw on Ervin's discussion of Mary Rose O'Reilly's work in teaching nonviolence. Both love and magic wind through these pages. These rhetorics swirl together lives and words, entirely not of my doing but nonetheless discoveries I made, or perhaps I should say "appearances" that have emerged so steadily that after a while I wasn't even surprised any more.[3] And so, a series of magical "reveals": Elizabeth Ervin memorializes Corder, noting the date of his death as 29 August 1998, sixteen years before Susan Lundy Maute would die, also on 29 August. Elizabeth Ervin, herself, would ultimately leave us too soon as a result of breast cancer, just like Sue, both of them mothers in their forties, both of them too young with much work yet to do. And Ervin joins Sue in the rejection of the battle metaphor, though of course the battle she refuses in her memorialization of Corder is one of scholarly proportions. She had not yet learned of her terminal breast cancer diagnosis at the time of that writing; it would come just a short stretch of years later. We gather together here in this last chapter to count our collective losses.

Ervin's ("Elizabeth" at times throughout this chapter, though sadly we never met) scholarly refusal enacts a grief over our public and private chasms. The "ridiculous" Jim Corder(s) haunts her: in memorializing him she traces our disciplinary limits, our ongoing refusals of both/ and in the academic and the personal. By the time she became ill, several years after this writing about her teacher, she published "There's

Nothing Good about Cancer" in her local newspaper, and in it she is rightfully, personally angry: "I thank cancer for nothing" (1). I find this piece and in particular its decidedly nonacademic forum an unspoken testament to the sorts of limits—subjectivities, textual spaces, genres— with which Ervin had long struggled. Exposing her own terminal illness, she makes a public call for further research, laments the inadequacy of insurance coverage, and openly mourns her losses of work, family, time. All the while she resists the pressure to behave according to culturally ascribed roles and expectations; she refuses to tidy up or to protect her audience emotionally or physically. In many ways Elizabeth embodies here much of what Sue and I both resisted and secretly grasped at around meaning and the hope for some sort of celestial comfort. She writes:

> I think there is an odd pressure placed on cancer patients to be gra-
> cious in their suffering: to reassure others of the truth behind such
> clichés as "everything happens for a reason" and of the continuing
> fairness of the universe. The demands of this role are too heavy for
> me, though. Contrary to popular myth, cancer is not ennobling; it
> brings me no peace, gives me no special insight into the workings of
> the cosmos. It compromises my dignity at every step. (1)

Sue was equally angry at her cancer but unwilling to concede its power, banning any appearance of it in word (no mention of breast cancer or her "battle" with it) or image (no trace of pink permitted) at her ser- vices, even denying the extent of her suffering: "It has not been hard. It's only been hard for the past nine months. I have lived a full, fun, crazy life. Nine months is going to dictate the whole rest of the bullshit? No" (Maute, "What I Want").[4] Though perhaps from other sides of the same room, both Sue and Elizabeth push against the roles they see as written onto them by a consuming set of public assumptions about breast cancer. In so doing, of course, they must carve out a kind of space, take a position of sorts, though that can come as a mixed refusal: "The demands of this role are too heavy for me." Sue dismisses—*no pink anything, anywhere!*—while Elizabeth acknowledges—*it compromises my dignity at every step.*

The idea of taking a position is fundamental to how we orient to the work we do (including what we choose *as* our work), to the construction of our subjectivity as language users and learners, and ultimately to the work itself, what might emerge from our positionality.[5] My goal in this chapter is to offer others interested in doing similar kinds of work a set of "thinking through" frameworks that might support the process. But

I want to begin by locating the origins of boundary-pushing, "scary," or destabilizing kinds of research and writing work in desire and its frustration. What I find most crucial in Sue and Elizabeth's positioning or orientation toward their cancers, respectively, is a mix of longing and inadequacy. Desire seeps through the lines: for hope, connection, cure, memory, vengeance, relief. While terminal illness magnifies urgently such desire, it simultaneously frustrates and denies. In so doing, in pulling and pushing us at once, its roots stretch wider and deeper, making room for us to think reflexively about what might emerge in the generative space of such frustrated desire and loss. In using terminal illness as a kind of metaphor or lever for academic work, my goal is not to undermine the real pain and real loss it renders; I have lived and continue to live with those. But I want to also respond to what I see as the creative potential, the unique learning that is possible when we reside in confounding spaces.

Ervin expressed a longing for more complex writing practices that broke traditional academic conventions far in advance of her cancer diagnosis and in ways that make her memorializing of Corder all the more urgent. Here I will call upon my own correspondence—one of the extracurricula of this book—with Lisa Ede, who remembers the following about a panel discussion at the first Feminisms and Rhetorics Conference:

> At one point Elizabeth asked very pointed questions about the limitations of scholarly writing. She wanted to write personally, to challenge academic norms. . . . But she was an untenured assistant professor early in her years. In my memory, the gist of her question/comment expressed the hope that because she was at a feminist conference— the first explicitly feminist conference in rhetoric-composition—she would get support for that desire. But of course she didn't because we all knew the realities of tenure and publishing. This discussion is the strongest memory (visual and kinesthetic) that I have of the conference because it so clearly made visible the patriarchal norms and constraints of the academy, one that even feminists couldn't in good conscience encourage Elizabeth to resist. It was a hard but illuminating moment, and she was really courageous in expressing her desire to challenge academic business as usual. ("Re: Feminisms and Rhetorics")

As the first Feminisms and Rhetorics Conference was held in 1997, by 1999 (when her memorial piece for Corder would be published) Ervin's frustration over how to represent Corder—"as 'Jim,' the man, or as 'Corder,' the academic"—is no surprise, to say nothing of what must have been her disappointment given "the patriarchal norms and constraints of the academy, one that even feminists couldn't in good conscience encourage Elizabeth to resist." Thus in memorializing Corder soon after this conference experience, Ervin's focus on his essay "Argument as Emergence, Rhetoric as Love," with its emphasis on how we might "transcend . . . rhetorical impasses," strikes me as a hopeful response to the refusal of her feminist colleagues to encourage her to "challenge academic business as usual" (Ervin, "Love" 323). How might, Ervin wonders, we operate differently? If we have indeed lost our taste for blood, what might we desire and why? What could our new exigencies be if not a push into battle? And, of course, what might we render in text? How might we come to our work, to our writing, to knowledge making when we decide "the demands of this role"—that of the stoic exemplar, the brave fighter, the cosmic guide, the coherent sage, the rational scholar—"are too heavy for me"? How might a love rhetoric, that which holds together "irreconcilable oppositions," help us dodge the hurtling asteroid(s) of our many invitations to battle?

In Situ: Pain and Possibility in Meeting Ourselves Where We Are At

This chapter is titled "in situ" after the most "ideal" breast cancer diagnosis, "ductal carcinoma in situ," where cancerous cells are located in the milk duct and have not spread to other parts of the body ("Mayo Clinic"). Oncologists typically recommend treatment for ductal carcinoma in situ and outcomes are generally good, though there is always the chance of recurrence. In the field of anthropology, an artifact found "in situ" is one

> that has not been moved from its original resting place or the place where it was deposited. Being in situ is critical to the interpretation of an artifact and to the circumstances that influenced its history. Once the location where an artifact is found is carefully documented, the artifact can be moved for conservation, additional analysis, or display. An artifact that is not discovered in situ is considered out of context and will not provide an accurate picture of its historical context. ("Secret in the Cellar")

The anthropological use of the term resonates with the medical through this notion of situatedness: in order to understand the thing itself, we must examine its roots or location and all the borders and limits that make up that space. An artifact studied out of context lacks value, meaning, even as it is itself limited by its containment. This definition inspired the previous subheading, "meeting ourselves where we are at," which is an homage to one of my great teachers, Eli Goldblatt. Eli has, on numerous occasions, reminded me to "meet students where they are at" in our many conversations about how to teach writing. This book, with its chapters titled in reverse "order," from a terminal diagnosis (stage IV) to that which is ideally manageable, refuses normative progressions or expected trajectories. We have instead worked backward in order to arrive at a place to begin, informed by the far reaches of where we might go or could have traveled. Our "where we are at"—*in situ*—is thus marked by all that is possible.

And so: when we assess our location at any given moment, we may uncover plenty of unbecoming realities. Instead of abandoning place, situation, or location, the task here becomes to work from the space and moment in which we find ourselves. I am reminded of lines from Susan Miller's *Textual Carnivals* that I printed out and taped to the inside of my office door when I started my first job as an assistant professor:

> The remaining comment about prejudice offers an interesting twist on the denigration of composition specialists perceived as the "rude proletariat." To what appears to be a theoretical contrary, this respondent said his department's "greatest tension is from the hot shot Marxist theorists. . . . They are new, have little time for day-to-day work of the department, carry all the prejudices of their corrupt elders, and speak to graduate students about composition and teaching in tones that say 'if you put your fingers in that shit, they will never come clean again.' They have no way of speaking about what we do." (247)

I am thinking now about what is at stake in our disavowals and our exnominations (Dolmage's "not me").[6] Do our wishes for wholeness or cleanliness every really get granted (and who does such granting, anyway)? What if it is true that my fingers will never come clean again? Can we—*must* we?—ever really escape the shit that marks us? In other words, what if "where we are at" is indeed *bad*? Why might we work from this place of badness? *In situ* is a call for staying put, valuing our location in badness: the undesirable places, the discomforts, the shame, and the spaces of loss, even anger. My hope is that this project offers one effort to work out of such a place and encourages others to do the same and on their own terms.

In his 1982 "On Cancer and Freshman Composition, or the Use of Rhetorical Language in the Description of Oncogenetic Behavior," Corder's assertion that, rhetorically at least, "we all . . . already have cancer" (6) is an invitation to experience ourselves as not only perpetually at risk and vulnerable but also capable of the activist potential in my favorite lines from Susan Miller. I do find Corder's work with rhetorical cancer problematic, particularly in his insistence that "cancer vanishes" if we can just make room for difference and disagreement; this I find far too naive and too eager for the kind of control cancer tends to eradicate. But I do think he's right about what is necessary regardless:

> However right or useful it might be, no information or insight can be appropriated into a person's inventive world unless there is a place for it (an emptiness waiting, or a need) or unless it can hook onto something already familiar. (6)

Cancer is embodied metaphor, not a foreign invader but rather a part of us run rampant.[7] For Corder the foundational idea here is that we see our own inherent cancers, our already existent "emptiness waiting, or a need" or "something already familiar." In a letter she wrote to her cancer, Sue—who often used to say to me anecdotally, "My body made this"—questions her cancer similarly ("Why have you decided to 'wake up'?") and expresses a wish for coexistence that resonates with Corder (and with Ervin's earlier resistance to battle):

> I don't want to die . . . apparently you don't want to either . . . so can we come to a place where we can live in harmony? Why do we have to fight to the death? Why does it have to be an "either or" situation? (Maute, "Hello Cancer")

Corder's hope for rhetorical balance or a kind of mutual regard—"such enfolding extended, no person, no cell, no flesh is alien, and cancer vanishes"—problematically wipes away fear and difference ("On Cancer" 8). However, in our embrace of an "emptiness waiting" we accept those things we do not yet know, those that perhaps are always threatening us but have gone thus far unseen or unheard, or perhaps the possibilities that are out of our control. We also come to terms with our own lack: of knowledge, of experience, of indestructability, of ability. To do feminist rhetorical work from this place means that we embed in our writing, research, and activism a continuous capacity for alienation, the expectation, however slight, for the breakdown of what might seem inevitable or otherwise predictable. Honoring Susan Miller and the importance of *Textual Carnivals* to the field at the 2016 Conference on College Composition and Communication, Jacqueline Rhodes writes that "Miller's textual subjectivity" seeks "a balance of opportunity and constraint" through which the subject occupies "a fictionalized stability, a temporary performativity" (4). Miller casts, for Rhodes, a kind of tension and fragility around the writerly subject, who "claim[s] fixed existence only in grounded and conventional lines on a page" (qtd. in Rhodes, "Susan Miller" 4). As such an existence is localized, momentary, and thus always vulnerable; it is also always to a certain extent unreal. My sense is that working "in situ" is laden with myriad contradictory tensions, at once situated and also potentially diffuse, both known and yet not fully known, much like the cancer such a diagnosis represents. Rhodes explains the project of "queering Susan Miller" as one that enacts the queer concept of disidentification, which for Judith Butler is the "uneasy sense of standing under a sign to which one does and does not belong" (qtd. in Rhodes, "Susan Miller" 7). Failure to work within or at least aware of this frame threatens to make the subject "more dependent and attached . . . to the idea of its coherence and power" (Musser qtd. in Rhodes 6). Rhodes asks us this foreboding disciplinary question: "Don't we see that today, as we celebrate 'naming what we know' in the field in order to proclaim ourselves a coherent, 'official' discipline?" (6).[8] To the extent that I can imagine "naming what we know" to be necessary work, it must also always be temporary, fragile work. We all need a place to begin. We are wrong, however, to believe that where we are is also all there is or that any singular location is fully stable. The task becomes to operate out of a location with this tension and uncertainty always in play.

No rhetorical display—in our writing, in how we do our research, or in how we canonize our terminology—will fully eradicate our potential for incoherence or instability. And as frightening as those dark corners may be, and indeed as awful as the reality of cancer in fact is, my work here is to assert and enact the value of these very spaces of uncertainty and risk. Our fingers will never come clean: the shit that marks us, that casts doubt on what we might wish we could know for sure, is a site rich for feminist rhetorical work. My sense is that Elizabeth Ervin hears in Corder's "Argument as Emergence, Rhetoric as Love" the inseparability of hope from uncertainty. She quotes him accordingly in the memorial piece: "Everything waits," he wrote. "Rhetorics mostly do not vanish, though they may lie hidden. . . . Everything is in progress, though we imagine it finished. Everything is exploratory, though we imagine it definitive" (Ervin, "Love" 326).

Who am I now that my life is consumed by disease? (Ervin, "There's Nothing Good")

When we examine ourselves, our writing, our research, and our research relationships both in situ and in love, we create a startling and essential tension. We must ask a series of questions that assess both our situatedness and our potential for movement, all at once: What is my place right here and right now? How did I arrive? How and where might I yet travel? What don't I know? In what ways am I potentially wrong? What is my fear? In a sense, this is a rhetoric for reflexive transformation, a reverse persuasion of sorts, though a persuasion nonetheless. Ervin explains:

> Focusing on how a rhetoric of love influences (persuades) *other people* might be missing the point. Perhaps it's more useful to focus on how it affects us. Speaking from my own experience, when I try to use language in this way—when I decline to participate in a "battle of words"—*I* become different. ("Love" 327)

In the face of terrifying or threatening possibilities or even realities, this move is embodied in Sue's "be okay": "And I don't know what that means. I don't know if that means like after I die or that I'm going to live another twenty years" (Maute, personal interview, 2 May 2014). But it is also Ervin's "who am I now" in this present, awful location—*in situ*—in the place of disease: How might I be remade? What does it mean to be someone I have never been before? Is it possible to be nothing at all? What have I lost and what have I gained? How might I change? This is an experience of subjectivity that happens in motion or exchange with others, against the grain of expectations, voiced and written and shared but ultimately delivered back to us anew. Considered the founding father of self-help or "pop" psychology, though historically a failed student of his own professed wisdom, M. Scott Peck offers us a resonant insight in his best-selling *The Road Less Traveled*, a way perhaps of thinking about Ervin's "rhetoric of love" as a unique agency, one independent of the limits of a weak or failing material body:

> When we grow, it is because we are working at it, and we are working at it because we love ourselves. It is through love that we elevate ourselves. And it is through our love for others that we assist others to elevate themselves. Love, the extension of the self, is the very act of evolution. It is evolution in progress. The evolutionary force, present in all of human life, manifests itself in mankind as human love.

Among humanity love is the miraculous force that defies the natural law of entropy. (267)

I become different.

Thinking Frames: Doing the Work That Undoes Us

As the driving argument of this book is that we make space for research and writing work that confounds or overwhelms us, I seek to avoid reductive or hierarchical boundary lines around methodology. Instead I maintain that we need attunement, the sort of sensitivity that allows us to recognize the projects that hold unique sway over us as writers, rhetors, and human beings, and we also need a set of frameworks that offers us ways to move within these projects. What follows is my best sense of such frameworks, at least as they have emerged in this project. I think of these as markers to support attunement, and to provide pathways in and through our work, despite or in light of the hovering power of the work itself. I do this in what follows by pulling forward themes from earlier in the book and then posing a series of applicable questions, which I expect will yield myriad responses reflective of the diversity of our work.

THE INTERSUBJECTIVE RESEARCH RELATIONSHIP

In her writing on surrender and intersubjectivity, Jessica Benjamin reminds us that "surrender is not To Someone . . . giving in or over to someone, an idealized person or thing" ("Intersubjectivity, Thirdness" 2). Rather, when we surrender into an experience with another we create the capacity to "explore . . . what just happened" in the dynamic between us, in our "sharing a pattern, a dance" (7). The emergence of this pattern is premised upon two core principles: rhythmicity and separateness. Both of these principles are fundamental and well established in rhetorical scholarship. Debra Hawhee's study of the classical link between athleticism and rhetorical education reminds us, again, of rhythmicity in an ancient wrestling manual: "The opponent's moves and the attention to specificity they require introduce difference to the repetition, demanding a new move between each of the throwing directives . . . demanding and producing its own kind of rhythmic response" ("Bodily Pedagogies" 149). As Hawhee indicates, rhythm depends upon separateness—"the opponent's moves and the attention to specificity they require"—and out of this collaboration, this dance, between two separate actors emerges a rhythm. Similarly, Stephanie Kerschbaum's work in disability rhetorics instructs us to understand difference as "dynamic, relational, and emergent" (57). My experience with Sue convinces me that embedding attention to both our rhythm and our separateness as an indelible component of method indeed becomes an act of knowledge making, generating ways of knowing and textual production constructed relationally and temporally.

But how do we recognize these unique dynamics? How do we nurture a safe space in which to balance rhythm and difference in our research collaborations? Many and diverse components may make up any one *dynamis*, as these possibilities shift depending upon circumstances. For Sue and me, the key components of our relationship are material, existential, and temporal. For example, as I reflect on our partnership, I must consider the following: In what ways did we, together and separately, orient to a sexed female maternal body? To what extent was this body a point of contact to which we would continuously return, a shared relational touchstone—for example, when she compared her distended abdomen to pregnancy, something she knew I had experienced—and in what ways might this touchstone also serve to experientially engage each of us in our respective, material divergence (for example: mastectomy)? "Material" of course is not limited to bodies but may also include texts, resources, even tools for use. The core question for moving through work in which we want to hold an intersubjective, collaborative energy between us must always be "In what ways do we at once meet here *and also* leave each other behind?"

This notion of "leaving each other behind" is sadly of paramount importance in any partnership marked by terminal illness. Accordingly, I include the "existential" as a consistent presence potentially at play when the nature of our relationship, our dialogue and shared experience, pushes us to ask questions about existence, meaning, and purpose. These are the kinds of questions that drive Ervin's contention about loving rhetorics and the turn inward: "I become different." I see the tension created between us—that which generates questions that drive us self-reflexively back into ourselves—as fundamental to some of the most sophisticated kinds of rhetorical work we can do. Sue and I circled around the following questions: What happens after we die? What if there is nothing? What if in fact there *is* something? What might it be? Terminal illness became the catalyst that enforced our separateness and the nature of our respective relationships to these questions. While they felt more exploratory for me, less urgent though surely important and even intimidating, for Sue they were ever more pressing. She worked on—or perhaps I should say worked toward or through—these questions. When we came together around the composing of her last wishes, she dictated to me, "I know where I am going. I know what's happening to me" (Maute, "What I Want"). We met at a valuing of existential questions, thanks to a shared humanity, but we also decidedly split apart at this juncture, our respective distance from their urgency illuminated.

The passage of time threads its way through all aspects of any collaboration, and in an intersubjective research partnership, time either seems to elongate, to make possible via accumulation the deepening of intimacy, or to rush forward urgently, knocking aside niceties and shuttling us into a deep, even disconcerting relational engagement. Terminal illness, I might argue, somehow manages to feel both slow and furiously fast all at once. The point, really, is that our work might unhinge us from our traditional expectations about time—long or short—and what it might yield. The task then is to interrogate these expectations, to determine what sorts of value we assign to time and what we think it might proportionally deliver. Accordingly I want to reframe questions I explored earlier in the book as I think they can be applied across contexts: To what extent do we associate "time spent" with increasing clarity? In other words, do we expect that over time the problem we are studying should become simpler, more clear, more manageable, or easier to understand? To what extent do we tend to link longevity and legitimacy? In other words, do we associate the length of time spent on a project to be directly correlative with its quality and reliability? In what ways might a particular project undermine such associations? Terminal illness—and indeed much of the scariest, hardest kinds of research and writing work we can do—delivers some sobering lessons about time. Though we might tell our stories, we never own or master time as Thomas Newkirk hopes in *Minds Made for Stories*. Time itself does not heal our wounds, nor does it cure our illnesses. It instead allows us space in which to act, to question—as Benjamin reminds us—"What just happened here?," and then it nevertheless pushes us forward regardless of our answers, our questions, and our losses.

IMAGINING BADNESS: OUR DATA

While this book, with its consideration of the dying body, invites us to think about any "data" as a material body capable of destruction, unreliability, and decline, I want to offer a focused framework here to call for a valuing of "badness" in the data we handle. I locate the theoretical roots of this notion in Jessica Benjamin's frame for the healing of collective trauma, "I could never imagine/I could imagine": "Accepting badness is part of the journey for those who actually expose themselves to civil rights violations, collective trauma, and indeed horrors with the hope of witnessing or actually helping" ("Discarded" 3). In other words, in "accepting badness" in the name of collective healing, we push ourselves intellectually and emotionally beyond what we otherwise might reject as "unimaginable." The atrocities and horrors committed and suffered must, on either side of the infraction, become possible in order to create a shared space in which understanding and collaborative problem-solving can take place. Again, Benjamin captures this most profoundly when she describes a mother's effort to forgive her daughter's killer amid apartheid violence. The mother ultimately visits the killer's village and brings her own sleeping bag so as not to create the additional work of cleaning extra sheets for others. The killer's sister's disappointment becomes for Benjamin a testament to the need to traverse our lived, visceral disconnects: "'I did not intend to wash the sheets. I wanted to sleep in the sweat of the woman who forgave my brother'" ("Discarded" 9). Again, for Benjamin this is a move to overcome "bodily separation on which we found our dissociation from the other's pain" (9). This willingness to be in or with the body of another—for all its pain, its capacity for loss or destruction, or even for violence—so that our own body might be changed is of extraordinary importance to feminist rhetorical work. I am reminded of Rita Charon's contention that "porous transit" is possible for medical doctors who open themselves to their patients' narrative experiences of illness (220).

Our task here as researchers and writers is to integrate into our efforts at knowledge making the kinds of data that confound, frighten, or even repulse us. In many ways this is an exercise in subjecting what we otherwise might imagine to be stable—our belief systems, what we "know" for sure, our methods, our values, our bodies/texts—to the possibility of devastation. In the case of Sue and me, this meant that I had to experience my body in our partnership as capable of illness and decline: I could imagine, I *had* to be able to imagine, my body as vulnerable to what I was witnessing in her body. This is not the same as living another's experience or claiming to know what it is like to be someone else. Rather, this is a methodological move that welcomes uncertainty, weakness, or even awfulness as valued, usable data toward the generation of particular kinds of texts and knowledge. Perhaps the most poignant transitional moment to this end between Sue and me happened when she pointed out to me that I'd "do it the same way," by which she meant I would navigate terminal illness in my own body in ways that reflected similarly the reactions and choices she made during her illness. Whether or not she might be correct, central here for me is the challenge to imagine my body's capacity for devastating illness in ways that I had not been able to before. This rhetorical, conceptual shift was absolutely essential to the deepening of our relationship and also remains fundamental to the kind of production—text, method, knowledge—unique to our collaboration.

And so for those working in similar spaces—though the focus may be different—I want to offer a series of framing questions designed to help us identify and value "badness" in our data. While I've written these questions primarily from the researcher perspective, I think they can be explored collaboratively in the research partnership as well. In many ways, "accepting badness is part of the journey" necessitates working on uncertain edges, and these edges I think often pull together emotional, intellectual, ethical, and practical challenges. For example, does the data generated in this work disturb or frighten me? Do I feel at times help-less, where the accumulated data point to a problem or issue for which no one in the research partnership (researcher/researched) sees easy or obvious solutions? Does the trajectory of questioning increasingly occasion answers that are either absent or unanticipated by all involved? Does the emergent data in this project cause me to doubt my methods, my ability to understand, or my ability to bring the work to some sort of comprehensive, coherent conclusion? In other words, do I, at least in certain ways, feel less confident around and within the project than when we began our work? Finally, am I shaken as a human being in this work and by the data it generates? Do I question my beliefs, my values, or my intentions in and through this collaboration and project? It would be misleading to suggest that there is any simple way to respond to these hard questions. Indeed, a simple process would undermine the pur-poses and possible outcomes inherent in more challenging, destabilizing work. Accordingly, my conviction here is that we write and talk our way through such questions over and over again (and that this process be as collaborative as possible within the research partnership), allowing our responses to complicate and shift over time and thus generate texts that mirror the uncertainty and risk inherent in doing such work in the first place. Sue assigned me the role of "keeper" of many recorded interviews and written artifacts with the charge that she would want to "be known" but that I keep private anything "that would hurt anyone."

I expect that I will continue to wrestle with my own uncertainty about my choices, even as I have thoughtfully made them.

RADICAL PASSIVITY: CUTTING AS OUR WORK

Two key reference points serve to shape the framework of radical passivity that I see as emergent in this project: Shannon Walters's exploration of rhetorical touch and Jack Halberstam's reading of Yoko Ono's *Cut Piece*. Walters's opening metaphor, that of Helen Keller's longtime teacher, Anne Sullivan, physically cutting and then reassembling Keller's written text into a more "linear narrative," captures the generative, complex, and simultaneously destructive tension at root in a rhetorical process of co-construction (27). Such co-construction requires a disassembling or taking apart of what Keller describes as her initial effort to "put my pieces together this way and that," in order to render what is ultimately a cocreated product (qtd. in Walters 26). In many ways this process resonates with the relational dynamics Benjamin describes in a "crash": "falling apart and coming back together as a usable object" ("Crash" 383). For Benjamin, impasse and rupture in the intersubjective partnership creates the opportunity for a generative recovery, the making for each of us some new way of being, a new identity in relation to the other. This change is not without loss: we cannot retain all of what we were before, much in the way Keller's written text ultimately came to be reassembled newly in ways that altered its meaning. Halberstam's reading of Ono's *Cut Piece*, which I've explored at multiple junctures throughout this book, where the performance artist invites audience members to physically cut away pieces of her clothing as her body is increasingly exposed, suggests a similar kind of transformation. For Halberstam, Ono embodies "radical passivity," a "feminism that fails to save others or to replicate itself, a feminism that finds purpose in its own failure" (128). In the context of my collaboration with Sue, these very generative notions of crashing and cutting happened amid our surrendering into change; they were not simply submissive. Ultimately I found myself unwilling to protect myself from her decline—*I am where I want to be*—and the inevitable loss it would impart on me. For both Ono and Keller, this embodied choice to be acted upon and ultimately changed is clear: the "text" is offered up by its original creator, its subject, to be taken apart, further exposed, and ultimately rendered newly, meaningfully.

But ultimately someone must do the cutting, and I would argue that at certain moments we each occupy such a place of power and even potential violence. Our task then as researchers and writers becomes twofold: while we must consider our own gaps and losses, what we have offered up and how this cutting away remakes us, we must conversely also examine our identity as cutters and the damage we have done.[9] We must work within a series of double-sided questions: What have we lost in the course of this work that was once familiar? In other words, what aspects of my thinking, my methods, my texts have gone from stable to unstable? Why? To what extent have I offered my "self"—as writer, as researcher, as human, as text itself—up for cutting? How attached am I or have I been to what or who I used to be and why? At the same time we must hold ourselves accountable as actors, ourselves cutters, and so the double-sided nature of these questions invites consideration of how we have cut, what choices we have made, and how these cutting moves come with inherent risks of damage. For example, in my work of representation and the myriad choices I have made among numerous rhetorical artifacts, how have I cast my research participant as vulnerable, partial, or weak? How and why have I exposed her, and how am I also changed and represented with this move? In the context of this project, my decisions to depict Sue's illness and in particular the increasing devastation of her body weigh heavily on me. I assume extraordinary power as "cutter" in detailing the realities of her illness and its relevancy to our collaboration, its capacity for meaning, and this is true even though she assigned me full permission to write about any of it. Despite even my care or good intentions, in what ways might I have hurt her, reduced her to her disease, or objectified her suffering? And perhaps equally significant, with each decision in what ways do I change, in terms of role and its boundary lines, the text I am able to create, the claim to knowledge I advance? These are meant to be hard questions attuned to the kinds of work that expose the vulnerability of both "researched" and "researcher." In fact I would argue that our work involves contending with the ways in which we are perpetually in concert, a *dynamis* in motion.

OWNING OUR MISFIT TOOLS

A clear sign that we are working in dark, uncertain spaces, that we are doing work that stands to overwhelm us, is the failure of our traditional tools to perform as we might expect. This does not make our tools insignificant; instead I might argue that they become more fully rhetorical. For me, this phenomenon is embodied metaphorically in Richard Miller's description of his father's suicide attempt, which I explored earlier in the book. Miller describes his father's particular struggle to explain his choice of a hammer: "At a loss for words, he could only say that he had felt at the time that it 'might have been of some use'" (265). Miller notes the "relative inaccessibility of this logic" in his father's explanation. In contrast, Miller exposes his own performance of rationality, his seemingly controlled capacity for delivering or packaging this story of lived experience, "the speaker at the podium, the performance of a masterful reading" (266). In juxtaposing these moments, Miller invites us to resist the clean distance between rationality and madness, between mastery and chaos. There is no safe side of the room when we take up work that insists we accept that "badness is part of the journey."

In this project, the most clearly misfit tool is likely my audio recorder, an instrument symbolic of traditional research that holds multiple, contradictory meanings in my relationship with Sue. On the one hand and to the extent that she associated it with formalized, traditional research, my audio recorder symbolized a kind of assigned "value" or importance to Sue's lived experience of illness. I often had it with me for our many conversations, though there were instances where I found it either unnecessary or inappropriate, or I completely forgot about it as the currents of our relationship and her illness eclipsed any thought of record keeping. At the same time, I invited direction from Sue regarding my recording of our conversations and found often that it mattered to her, that she wanted to confirm that I had indeed "gotten that down." On one occasion we were out to lunch and I had forgotten both recorder and notebook, my traditional researcher tools, and she dug into her purse and handed me her last bloodwork results, instructing me to "write on the back" and making certain I had a pen before she continued.[10] Still, I want to hold amid this assigned importance my own hesitancy and forgetting, the ways in which I found my recorder at times awkward, potentially intrusive, a violation of our intimacy or her privacy. And so when I read—after the fact—Gesa Kirsch's warning, "Close friends do not usually arrive with a tape-recorder, listen carefully and sympathetically to what you have to say and then disappear," I experienced immediately a kind of panic or shame around my use of this distant, cold tool (Cotterill qtd. in Kirsch 2166). However, and as I have considered at earlier points in the book, my use of the recorder was inconsistent with the final move of the recorder-wielding researcher Kirsch imagines: disappearance. And so in what ways might meaning, or the notion of how we do research or why we collect data, shift when we use our tools out of step, unpredictably? And to what extent does our anxiety about our research tools, our uneasy awareness of their potential for misfit and misuse, indicate our arrival at overwhelming, intimidating, or even frightening kinds of work? What are our ethical obligations at these junctures, and how and why might we responsibly stay with such projects even as we contend with our own uncertain movements?

Mourning: Anticipatory Grief and Last Rites

Love feels more and more like the only subject.
—*Salman Rushdie, "February 1999"*

There is nothing easy here. Loving rhetorics, reluctant to do battle and instead reaching both outward and inward, can expose our failures to perform, reveal our ignorance and limitations, and showcase our activist queering of the inevitable—*and I don't know if that means like after I die or if I'm going to live another twenty years*—and when we disidentify we sometimes make our stance public in ways that invite a kind of public shaming. We may react defensively on our weaker days (that's when we cover up or wish we could indeed vanish), retreating entirely and thus losing our activist edge, and some of us get angry. For Patti Lather, as we know, the anger comes when she's asked about crying: "Why the need to know I cried?" (211).[11] For Lather, her audience's interest in her grief over the loss of her research participants to HIV/AIDS represents the "Oprah-ization of this era of confessional talk," and what Lather perceives as her audience's desired response, the "'validity of tears,'" is a source of "great discomfort" (211).[12] Ervin anticipates as much when she ponders the professional shamefulness of "loving rhetorics": "Is it because love itself has been Oprahfied beyond recovery?" (322). Lather's solution in *Troubling the Angels* is to craft an "undramatized, largely effaced narrative presence" (211).

Such a move stands to strip subjectivity in the face of work that—if we are being honest—hurts and scares and confuses us. Lather and Ervin, writing in the late 1990s, both indicate the ways in which "the confessional" has been commodified, *Oprahfied* and *Oprah-ized*, and thus cheapened in spaces of professional authority, validity, reliability. As I write years later I have discovered that Oprah now offers us a feature on her website, "things I know for sure," a move of her own that seems to respond to a similar longing among her constituents.[13] We are invited to find solace in twenty of Oprah's top maxims, including "What you put out comes back all the time, no matter what" and "You define your own life. Don't let other people write your script" ("Top 20"). Belief is a human longing and a need. It also always stands to colonize the confessional—in many ways a mode that Oprah herself had packaged as entertainment by the time of Lather's and Ervin's writing—particularly when our confessions demonstrate our failures of belief, our status on the outskirts of acceptable behavior as defined by the signposts of our professions, our dominant communities and codes.[14]

What is the impact of Lather's subjectivity on an ethnography that follows a support group of women living and dying with an awful disease? What kind of book does a "largely effaced narrative presence" render? *Troubling the Angels* experiments with nontraditional form in ways that are surely exciting still: each page is broken into competing genres, at times offering practical information and at others telling participants' stories. But in her 2008 review, Dorte Marie Søndergaard finds that the authors have perhaps "moved too softly and obliquely" (33). Explaining the book's driving metaphor, a pair of angel's wings with one wing signifying the "non-understandable" and the other that which "belongs to the world," Søndergaard laments that the authors have left "too much space" around the wing that lies "beyond the world and the rational." Rather, for Søndergaard, "both wings have to move simultaneously if the metaphor is to work, and I here I miss more strength and integration in the analytical voices of the authors" (33).

Integration is grueling and loving rhetorical work. Ervin explains the particular difficulty involved when our integration efforts demand intimacy and thus a clouded, more complicated view:

> But while it's easy to imagine "applications" of civic love to various unknown disenfranchised humans—the homeless, the AIDS-afflicted, the poor—it's less easy to direct it toward people we know, or know of, but don't much like. . . . That's what makes it hard—a discipline, even. ("Love" 327)

The discipline Ervin reaches for here is one premised on contradiction, on the failure of belief or conviction, and sometimes against the grain of what we might wish for (things like clarity, simplicity, rationality). Terminal illness ushers in a similar conundrum: its language undoes us, takes from us those we love, forces us to accept and to let go, at best to surrender into that which does not make easy sense. As we work (over and over again, I hope) in my field of rhetoric-composition to define ourselves as a *discipline*, what might Ervin's discipline look like? How might love render our writing, our research, our professional community, our knowledge as painfully ours to hold tight and also to perpetually lose? I maintain that we must count our losses as central to our work. Ervin's question remains: Is there any "principled means of yielding to others without being coopted or losing face" (322)? There will be casualties one way or the other, however we move.

A memory:

> My hand is on her back and I can feel every rib as I hold her up against my hip, angling her so she can dry heave into the trash can beside the bed. These are the last hours. I tell her to just let it go, just go with it, just let it happen. She retches but there is simply nothing left. We are still with this body but its actions seem at this point almost imaginary. She asks me how I am. I tell her I am exactly where I want to be. ("Reflection: Hospice")

I am still here. I stayed back then too and I am still here now. How might such a practice—*in situ*—invite us to also loosen ourselves from our constraints to learning and to writing? Might we surrender lovingly and radically into the idea that in any singular place we will have our limits and our losses, that we will see what we know or what we thought was right inevitably chipped away or redefined by those rhetorics that "may lie hidden"? That at some point or another, the structures and set of rules we have assembled won't work any more? My sense is that the application of such questions to our work will yield diverse responses; there isn't a singular genre or conclusion that I expect to render here.

I also have no intention of casting a happy or overly optimistic ending for this book. We live in frightening times and have in the United States—as of this writing—elected a president who promises to "make America great again" with the erection of all sorts of walls. Many of us find we are outsiders. But in our human reaching toward what Rhodes reminds us is a "fictionalized stability" we inherit too an opportunity to disidentify, to sit in our fear or uncertainty, to build on our own "cloud[s] of doubt" as creative and generative ("Rhizomes"). We might testify to our losses and our pain, to our utter confusion, to our shit. Loving rhetorics make space for such strange movements, at once backward and forward. We can acknowledge that we've behaved irrationally. In her boldly angry piece for the local newspaper, Elizabeth Ervin writes,

> It is difficult to live a full life while contemplating life without me in it, and yet that's my challenge and I do my best to meet it. . . . Some days dreaming of the future feels a little like looking into the sun: linger too long and the image burns into nothingness. I do it anyway.

Don't ask me to be grateful for the opportunity. ("There's Nothing Good" 2)

I read Ervin's mix of indignation, subversion, and hopelessness to be an embodied, radical act of mourning. She is at once passive, having no gratitude for a dismal, unasked-for opportunity to stare "into nothingness," and yet also active: *I do it anyway.*

But, why?

Jessica Benjamin offers us a fraught explanation: "Harmony and dissonance are resolved by returning to the original note or chord, in which the power of the resolution depends on how much tension or dissonance is created" ("From Many into One" 198). What are the potentialities of our work at the highest levels of tension and dissonance? And what are the reasons for why we might pursue these most frightening kinds of projects, those that take us to our own edges, uncertain of how or whether we will return?

Stillness, passivity, indeed a falling away of the structures we always thought we could count on—including ourselves, our bodies, our methods, our texts, perhaps even "what we (think we) know"—are the core tenets of this book. Love, in all its senselessness, as academic, rhetorical work, as a research method, is just one more transgression. It is, however, *the* transgression that unlocks all the rest: it is the vehicle that makes subjective transformation possible. It changes us as researchers and writers and teachers and friends. It generously allows us to move despite the fact that, as Corder reminds us, "we can't help but stand somewhere," limited, unsophisticated animals that we are (qtd. in Ervin, "Love" 324). I think about where I once stood: agreeing to write down my friend's wishes while steadfastly resisting the belief that she would soon be gone. Over our two years of writing and talking about her illness, my helping Sue come to terms with her death shuttled me forward into my own irrevocable loss. Perhaps Oprah's assertion that "what you put out comes back all the time, no matter what" is at least sometimes correct. One day in July, a little over a month before her death and following a particularly awful night spent in the hospital, I received a text message, a featured "Bloodwork" earlier in the book, from Sue: "Very interesting morning . . . I'm doing well. Interesting in a profound way. As heinous as my life looks on the outside, I love my life . . . and these feelings are without . . . morphine!" (Maute, "Re: Interesting morning").

I do it anyway.

Loving rhetorics renders research and writing work that resists coercion, simple acquiescence, or submission. I understand that, nevertheless, readers might need to rage against my insufficiencies and general reluctance here to assuage their own longings for stability (I have those same longings). I know I have written an imperfect book. Still: the trajectory of Ervin's writing casts an unfolding. Increasingly she must face how difficult these conceptual and rhetorical tensions are to uphold, that indeed the work of loving is at times painful, contradictory, and seemingly irrational.[15] In this receptive, respectful dance, we discover the "real value," according to Ervin, of "a loving rhetoric" ("Love" 327). Should we believe in such foolish, irrational magic, we would be wise to gather up our losses and expose the holes that also constitute us, wounds from the cutting-away of us and of what we thought we knew. We "become different"—and so then it *all* becomes different—but we likely will find that our friends are still with us.

I will end with a little story and a cut-up text. About a year before her death, Sue and I recorded an interview during one of her chemo treatments. We were in a large room, surrounded by patients receiving treatment, some of them very obviously ill. We had balanced my recorder on the armrest of the chair between us, curtains partially drawn, and I can remember how I scrambled intellectually to disconnect the visible sickness surrounding us from what was Sue's healthful appearance at the time. Her face was vibrantly rosy, and she was dressed to attend a concert that evening. Following her treatment she left the room with characteristically energetic, friendly goodbyes to the nurses, trailing me behind her, and I remember that we lingered a while outside in the hospital parking lot. She talked with some heaviness then about her frustrated sense of "direction": What could she do with the rest of her life? Who'd seriously hire her with terminal cancer? How could she help others? Where might she go from here? And with that, she dashed to her car and went off to enjoy some music with her family.

I thought about her questions all evening. Early the next morning I wrote her an email about this idea of "direction" and the ways she already embodied it: "That you could get that treatment, bound out of that ugly blue chair, and dash off to a concert . . . is all the direction any of us, whatever our situations, would be proud to attain" (Restaino, "Re: Direction"). I suppose in some ways this makes me think about how the potential for growth, "direction" if we might find some comfort in that word, rests sometimes in *staying with* our locations, *in situ*. In this sense, we need not go much of anywhere but right here, now, being with our various boundaries and circumstances, some of them seemingly glittering and others terribly vile, all of them ripe for some sort of digging in. Sue wrote me back:

> Thank you for your message . . . and I have struggled with my "purpose" and wondering how I can contribute to the world given my limiting situation. . . . I do want to help others, and I do think I have some positive and helpful things to share with others, it's just figuring out how to do that. . . . You make a great observation, and one that has given me some food for thought. . . . It's a new way of looking at a current "problem" for me. And to be honest, it's really how the universe tells us to live our lives. Instead of moving toward your "dreams," you are supposed to come from your dreams and live as if these dreams, wishes, desires are already happening. To feel them. To be them. Moving towards your dreams, you never really get there. . . . Coming from them and feeling as if they are already happening, more than likely changes your reality. I keep waiting for it to look a certain way, but maybe I stop looking for this "aha" moment and, instead, continue to live as fully as I have with each day that comes.
>
> I guess my issue becomes, how to make my "message" known to those who could benefit from it. Your email has really given me a new outlook, seriously . . . a sense of peace in many ways, like I don't have to do any more than what I am already doing. (Maute, "Re: Direction")

NOTES

WORKS CITED

INDEX

NOTES

A Necessary Scan. Beautiful Mess, Dark Energy: This Book

1. See especially Barbara Ehrenreich's "Smile! You've Got Cancer" and her book that same year, *Bright-Sided: How the Relentless Promotion of Positive Thinking Has Undermined America.*

2. See "Surrender as Method: Research, Writing, Rhetoric, Love."

3. Special thanks go to my good friend Paula Mathieu for pushing me toward this tension in our discussions (and her insightful readings) of this project.

4. This intimacy must be cocreated and mutually vulnerable, as Michelle Fine's extraordinary essay, "Working the Hyphens: Reinventing Self and Other in Qualitative Research" teaches and challenges us.

5. There is a body of work in rhetoric-composition, too extensive to explore fully here, that informs my questions and has long considered the ethics and importance of archival and posthumous research and writing. See especially McKee and Porter's "Ethics of Archival Research"; Kirsch and Rohan's *Beyond the Archives*; and Shipka's ongoing work on embodiment, memory, and remediation, which continues to be intellectual fodder and inspiration.

6. See especially Hawke's *Counter-History of Composition.*

Stage IV. Making Space: Methodology
and the Search for Ourselves

1. Certainly Derrida's work on time, repeatability, event, and narrative is an important theoretical resource here, one to which I am not able to give ample attention but which informs my thinking.

2. See especially Carlo et al., "Hunting Jim W. Corder"; and Baumlin and Miller, *Selected Essays of Jim W. Corder.*

3. See especially Hawhee, *Bodily Arts.*

161

4. For more on this story, see "50 Stunning Olympic Moments No. 3: Derek Redmond and Dad Finish the 400m," *The Guardian*, 30 November 2011, https://www.theguardian.com/sport/blog/2011/nov/30/50-stunning -olympic-moments-derek-redmond (accessed 13 July 2016).

5. Of note here is Beth Daniell's work on women, friendship, and literacy outside the academy; see especially *A Communion of Friendship: Literacy, Spiritual Practice, and Women in Recovery*. See also William Rawlins's extensive work in communication studies.

6. Of worthy note here are divisions in breast cancer diagnosis and treatment for women across racial and socioeconomic categories. While this book does not take up such an investigation, I am certain that Sue's and my respective experiences of whiteness informed our relationship and our understanding of the treatment she received. For data on disparities in treatment and diagnosis across ethnic and socioeconomic groups, see the National Cancer Institute website.

7. There are a number of useful discussions of the role and history of expressivism in the field, and often with a particular emphasis on the role of expressivism and its shaping of composition pedagogy. The well-known "Bartholomae/Elbow" debate serves as a kind of tipping point for a move away from expressivism, though others have argued convincingly that, as a field, we have not ever fully made this departure (or, that while our scholarship has left discussions of expressivism increasingly unspoken, our approach to teaching has retained it). See especially Eli Goldblatt's essay "Don't Call It Expressivism: Legacies of a 'Tacit Tradition.'"

8. See especially Corder, "Tribes and Displaced Persons."

9. Hephzibah Roskelly and Kate Ronald's book, *Reason to Believe: Romanticism, Pragmatism, and the Teaching of Writing*, examines Enlightenment thinking as a vehicle for instilling "belief" in the teaching of writing and repairing what the authors see as a theory/practice divide. For further discussions of Enlightenment thought in the field see also Faigley, "Literacy after the Revolution," and Rhodes's *Radical Feminism, Writing, and Critical Agency* for some critique of essentialism in relation to Enlightenment thought. Byron Hawke's excellent book *A Counter-History of Composition* examines the theoretical underpinnings of subjectivity, method, and the mind-body connection through an investigation of vitalism.

10. There is however an extensive body of such cancer narratives, including Audre Lorde's *Cancer Journals* and many others; also of note is emerging scholarship on breast cancer narratives as they unfold online. See especially Beemer, "From the Margins of Healthcare."

11. An exciting exception is *Reorienting Writing Studies: Queer Methods, Queer Projects*, edited by Caroline Dadas, Will Banks, and Matt Cox (forthcoming from Utah State University Press).

12. Feminist research methodologists have long called for reflexivity on the part of the researcher, and examples of such calls are too numerous to list here (see especially Harding's "standpoint theory" and Chiseri-Strater's notion of "turning in upon ourselves"). Despite these foundational contributions (and others), my argument seeks to push and build on this work toward greater attention to the transformation of the researcher-writer subject and its role in knowledge-making.

13. See Restaino and Maute, "Surrender as Method: Research, Writing, Rhetoric, Love."

14. This idea of "working by hand" has its roots in Goldblatt's "Making Charoset."

Stage III. Rooting Surrender: Rhythm, Dissonance, and Letting Go in the Research Process

1. Benjamin's treatment of "thirdness" and the notion of "surrender" has roots in the work of her mentor Emmanuel Ghent. See especially Ghent's "Masochism, Submission, Surrender." Worth exploration is also the exchange between Benjamin and Judith Butler; see especially Butler, "Longing for Recognition"; Benjamin, "Response to Commentaries by Mitchell and Butler"; and Benjamin, "Intersubjectivity, Recognition, and the Third: A Comment on Judith Butler."

2. My sources here are the *Oxford English Dictionary*, 2nd ed. (1989), and Dryden's translation of Virgil's *Georgics*.

3. For a useful and foundational collection on rhetoric and the body, see especially Crowley and Selzer, *Rhetorical Bodies*; see also Wells's *Our Bodies, Ourselves and the Work of Writing* and Howard's excellent "Embodiment, Machines, and the Posthuman."

4. Ghent was a pioneer composer of electronic music; for a summary of his accomplishments, see his *New York Times* obituary, "Emmanuel Ghent, 77, Composer, Innovator, and Psychoanalyst," 13 April 2003.

5. Counseling professionals have long argued for such end-of-life planning, though the actual process continues to be challenging for patients, professionals, and family members alike. See, for example, Narang et al., "Trends in Advance Care Planning in Patients with Cancer."

6. Ehrenreich's *Bright-Sided* is of course a major voice in this conversation, as Ehrenreich draws on her own breast cancer diagnosis and

treatment; see also and especially Orenstein's "Our Feel-Good War on Breast Cancer" and "The Wrong Approach to Breast Cancer."

7. I am informed theoretically by Derrida, whose work Lisa Mazzei uses as a frame for designing her own qualitative methodology in education research for "hearing" absences and silence; I spend focused attention on this work in the following chapter.

8. What I'm responding to here, in the context of the field of rhetoric-composition, is what I see more as a failure of synthesis and deliberative hybridization between methodologies than as an openly dismissive culture in how we do our work. My hope is that this observation might also resonate with scholars in disciplines outside of my field. I will spend more focused attention on this tension in the following chapter.

9. My discussion and quotation of my correspondence with Lisa Ede is done with her written permission.

10. In my use of the term "epistolary" I am informed by Sondra Perl's *On Austrian Soil*, which includes a series of difficult, deeply personal letters between Perl and her friend and former student Margret as they negotiate the painful cultural history of anti-Semitism that at once unites and separates them. I will give additional attention to Perl's work later in this book.

11. Those interested in further reading should see Benjamin's *Beyond Doer and Done To*, which follows this essay and also further develops the foundational ideas in *The Bonds of Love*; my own writing largely preceded the publication of *Beyond Doer* and so I am unable to give Benjamin's latest work fuller attention here.

12. See the first chapter of this book for a fuller discussion of Charon's work in narrative medicine.

13. My wary reference here is to ongoing conversations around threshold concepts in the field and the push to carve out a set of disciplinary terms, "what we know." While this push has integrity in its valuing of knowledge making in rhetoric-composition and the pursuit of a shared language for disciplinary practice, I find inherent here the paradoxical challenge of simultaneously retaining and protecting what I see as the core reality in the study of literacy, language, and our (researchers', teachers', students') struggle with words: that which, ultimately, we do not know.

14. My thinking here is informed by work in mobility studies and in particular by the 2016 Watson Conference, which took mobility as its theme. See especially the Sweetland Digital Rhetoric Collaborative site for reviews of select 2016 Watson presentations, http://www.digital rhetoriccollaborative.org/category/conference-reviews/other-reviews /watson-2016/.

Stage II. Building and Breaking: Methodological Contradictions and Unanswerable Questions

1. See especially Schell and Rawson, *Rhetorica in Motion*; see also Kirsch and Royster, *Feminist Rhetorical Practices*.

2. In fact in 2014 the Conference on College Composition and Communication Research Committee sponsored a panel, "Transparency in Research: Messiness, Rigor, and Ethics in the Conduct of Writing Research," which featured Smagorinsky as expert respondent.

3. Among the foundational work to this end in rhetoric-composition, see especially Chiseri-Strater's "Turning In upon Ourselves" and also Newkirk's "Seduction and Betrayal in Qualitative Research," both in Mortensen and Kirsch, *Ethics and Representation in Qualitative Studies of Literacy*.

4. See Glenn's *Unspoken*. See also Ratcliffe's *Rhetorical Listening*.

5. See especially Rickly's "Messy Contexts."

6. Relevant, foundational explorations in rhetorical theory are too numerous to discuss here, but the work of Kenneth Burke is essential to my own understanding of the incompleteness of language to convey respective experience.

7. See this book's preface for more about Feynman and his relevancy to this project.

8. I am not able to give significant attention to the extensive body of scholarship on trauma theory here; for foundational reading in trauma theory, see Herman's *Trauma and Recovery* as well as Van der Kolk's *Body Keeps the Score*. Scholarship in rhetoric-composition that draws on trauma theory has most recently been focused especially on working with veterans in the writing classroom; see Schell and Kleinbart's "'I Have to Speak Out': Writing with Veterans in a Community Writing Group" as well as the Syracuse Veteran's Writer's Group, founded and led by Schell.

9. A description of this workshop, as well as sample materials, can be found in the Fall/Winter 2016 issue of *Peitho*. I draw on some of that previously published description here.

Stage I. Radical Care: Rhetorical Bodies in Contact

1. This claim has its roots in the classical period, through Burke, and beyond and as such is far too expansive for sustained attention here. But again, see Rebecca Howard's foundational bibliography, "Embodiment, Machines, and the Posthuman," as a useful starting point. I do want to acknowledge here, even as my focus is on human beings and their rhetorical

agency, that there is also a long tradition of work on rhetorics and the nonhuman, and particularly in exploration of Native American cultures and symbol using to communicate across nonhuman sentient beings.

2. See especially foundational work by Nel Noddings, Sandra Harding, and, as related to the issue of research ethics, Ellen Barton, as well as Eileen Schell and Patricia L. Stock's exploration of women's status as workers in composition classrooms in *Moving a Mountain: Transforming the Role of Contingent Faculty in Composition Studies and Higher Education.*

3. So acute are these sensations that I am compelled to include a note here that Clarke coauthored this narrative with her adult daughter, who not only survived this attack but whose asthma had become more manageable by the time of their writing.

4. See the first chapter for a fuller exploration of Corder's thinking.

5. Dolmage offers a much fuller discussion of the theoretical underpinnings unique to this phenomenon of negativity or exnomination, drawing on a range of important critical voices, including Foucault and his notion of "biopower"; see especially the first chapter of *Disability Rhetoric*, "Disability Studies of Rhetoric," for this essential framing.

6. My use of "not me" has roots in Dolmage's "exnomination" but is also an acknowledgment of Harry Stack Sullivan's early interpersonal theory; for further discussion of Sullivan and his contributions, see Evans's *Harry Stack Sullivan.*

7. In many ways, this familiar/alien construction has theoretical roots in Freud's notion of the "uncanny," which he builds through exploration of the German *heimleich/unheimleich*, meant to represent that which is both "of the home" and also concurrently entirely "strange" or "unfamiliar." To the extent that the experience of terminal illness can be considered a trauma—both for the ill and for those who love them—the experience can render some version of the uncanny, recognition and alienation housed within the same/familiar body.

8. I'm reminded of course of Susan Sontag's famous *Illness as Metaphor* in which she advances a very different sort of argument about the tendency toward "victim blaming" as an explanation for serious illness; here I am moving to make use of illness—and so in that way I suppose objectifying illness to a certain extent—as a vehicle by which we might think and work more radically.

9. I discuss this presentation and events surrounding the conference more fully in the opening chapter, "A Necessary Scan."

10. For a useful discussion of agonistic rhetoric, see especially Roberts-Miller's *Deliberate Conflict.*

11. I give fuller attention to Halberstam, including the notion of "radical passivity," in "Stage III, Rooting Surrender."

12. See also Clare's book, *Exile and Pride*.

13. See especially "On Cancer and Freshman Composition."

In Situ. Love as Frame

1. In many ways this experience is taken up in disability studies via the term "supercrip" and also Stella Young's "inspiration porn"; see especially Young's 2014 TED talk for a popular application of these concepts in the context of disability activism.

2. I have in mind as I write these words Adrienne Rich's essential essay "When We Dead Awaken: Writing as Re-vision" in which Rich calls for a feminist reseeing of texts, meaning, and literary representation.

3. I'm a bit haunted here by Carl Jung's term "synchronicity," which he describes as a "meaningful coincidence" or as an "acausal connecting principle"; for Jung's first formal writing on the subject see his 1952 "Synchronicity: An Acausal Connecting Principle," which has been reissued in multiple collections of Jung's writings. My thanks to Rosemarie Ciccarello for first pointing me in this direction.

4. I visit and revisit the experience of coauthoring Sue's wishes throughout the book; the "Stage III" chapter marks the introduction of this event though again its significance is threaded throughout.

5. Worthy of note here is the concept of feminist standpoint theory, advanced by Sandra Harding and others, which comes with a long history of debate among feminist scholars. I am unable to engage these debates here, though I recognize my own project as both engaging in and dissenting from aspects relevant to these debates; for further reading, see Harding's edited collection, *The Feminist Standpoint Theory Reader*.

6. See especially the "Stage I" chapter for a longer discussion of Dolmage's use of this term.

7. Here I'm immediately reminded again of the title of Susan Sontag's essential work, *Illness as Metaphor*, to which I am unable to pay due attention but which I have held in mind throughout this work.

8. Rhodes's reference here is to the popular book coedited by Linda Adler-Kassner and Elizabeth Wardle, *Naming What We Know: Threshold Concepts of Writing Studies*, which attempts to articulate thirty-seven "shared beliefs" in order to "name what we know" in the field of rhetoric-composition (xix).

9. I want to acknowledge a conceptual or at least terminological overlap with "cutting" as a practice (the clinical term is "non-suicidal self-injury"

or NSSI), most commonly as a response to emotional pain or psychological numbness; while I am not exploring NSSI here I do hold this practice in mind as a potentially rich site for further consideration. My thanks to Jackie Rhodes for pointing out this connection at the 2017 Feminisms and Rhetorics Conference.

10. I recount this moment in my essay "Surrender as Method."

11. Lather coauthored *Troubling the Angels: Women Living with HIV/AIDS* with social worker Chris Smithies; here she writes reflectively about her own relationship to the project in an essay, "Postbook: Troubling the Ruins of Feminist Ethnography."

12. I discuss Lather's work and this moment in particular with greater attention in the "Stage I" chapter.

13. I want to point at the possible nod here toward Dorothy Allison's memoir, *Two or Three Things I Know for Sure.*

14. This is foundational Foucault; I do not believe full engagement here is necessary, but nevertheless this tension is worthy of our continued attention.

15. In "Elizabeth Ervin and the Challenge of Civic Engagement: A Composition and Rhetoric Teacher's Struggle to Make Writing Matter," David Gold charts the course of Ervin's scholarly arc, one in which she pursues doggedly her devotion to civic rhetorics and the writing classroom as an engaged space while also rethinking her choices, exposing her own failures, refining her stance and approach.

WORKS CITED

Adler-Kassner, Linda, and Elizabeth A. Wardle. *Naming What We Know: Threshold Concepts of Writing Studies*. Utah State UP, 2015.

Allison, Dorothy. *Two or Three Things I Know for Sure*. Penguin, 1996.

Anderson, Erika. "Tinged Pink: When the Cancer Narrative Can't Compass Your Loss." *Gawker*, 25 Oct. 2014.

Bartholomae, David. "Writing with Teachers: A Conversation with Peter Elbow." *College Composition and Communication*, vol. 46, no. 1, 1995, pp. 62–71.

Barton, Ellen. "Further Contributions from the Ethical Turn in Composition/Rhetoric: Analyzing Ethics in Interaction." *College Composition and Communication*, vol. 59, no. 4, 2008, pp. 596–632.

Baumlin, James S., and Keith D. Miller. *Selected Essays of Jim W. Corder: Pursuing the Personal in Scholarship, Teaching, and Writing*. NCTE, 2004.

Beemer, Christy. "From the Margins of Healthcare: De-mythicizing Cancer Online." *Peitho: Journal of the Coalition of Feminist Scholars in the History of Rhetoric and Composition*, vol. 19, no. 1, 2016, pp. 93–127.

Benjamin, Jessica. *Beyond Doer and Done To: Recognition Theory, Intersubjectivity and the Third*. Routledge, 2017.

———. *The Bonds of Love: Psychoanalysis, Feminism, and the Problem of Domination*. Pantheon Books, 1988.

———. "Crash: What We Do When We Cannot Touch: Commentary on a Paper by Meira Likierman." *Psychoanalytic Dialogues*, vol. 16, no. 4, July/Aug. 2006, pp. 377–85.

———. "The Discarded and the Dignified, Parts 1–6." *Public Seminar: The New School for Social Research*, Dec. 2014, www.publicseminar.org/2014/12/the-discarded-and-the-dignified-parts-1-and-2. Accessed 17 Jan. 2017.

———. "From Many into One: Attention, Energy, and the Containing of Multitudes." *Psychoanalytic Dialogues*, vol. 15, no. 2, 2005, pp. 185–201.

———. "Intersubjectivity, Recognition, and the Third: A Comment on Judith Butler." *Judith Butler: Padagogische Lekturen*, edited by Norbert Ricken and Nicole Balzer, VS Verlag fur Sozialwissenschaften, 2012, pp. 283–301.

———. "Intersubjectivity, Thirdness, and Mutual Recognition." Talk given at the Institute for Contemporary Psychoanalysis, Los Angeles, CA, 2007, icpla.edu/wp-content/uploads/2013/03/Benjamin-J.-2007-ICP-Presentation-Thirdness-present-send.pdf. Accessed 17 Jan. 2017.

———. "Response to Commentaries by Mitchell and Butler." *Studies in Gender and Sexuality*, vol. 1, no. 3, 2000, p. 308.

Bizzell, Patricia. *Feminist Historiography in Rhetoric*. Rhetoric Society, 2002.

Blankenship, Lisa. "Changing the Subject: A Theory of Rhetorical Empathy." Diss., U of Miami, 2013.

Buber, Martin. *Pointing the Way: Collected Essays*. Edited and translated with an introduction by Maurice S. Friedman, Harper Brothers, 1957.

Burke, Kenneth. *A Rhetoric of Motives*. U of California P, 1969.

Butler, Judith. "Longing for Recognition: Commentary on the Work of Jessica Benjamin." *Studies in Gender and Sexuality*, vol. 1, no. 3, 2000, pp. 271–90.

———. *Precarious Life: The Powers of Mourning and Violence*. Verso, 2004.

Carlo, Roseanne, et al., eds. "Symposium: Hunting Jim W. Corder." *Rhetoric Review*, vol. 32, no. 1, 2013, pp. 1–26.

Charon, Rita. *Narrative Medicine: Honoring the Stories of Illness*. Oxford UP, 2006.

Chiseri-Strater, Elisabeth. "Turning In upon Ourselves: Positionality, Subjectivity, and Reflexivity in Case Study and Ethnographic Research." *Ethics and Representation in Qualitative Research Studies*, edited by Gesa Kirsch and Peter Mortensen, NCTE, 1996, pp. 115–32.

Clare, Eli. *Exile and Pride: Disability, Queerness, and Liberation*. South End Press, 1999.

Corder, Jim W. "Aching for a Self." *Selected Essays of Jim W. Corder: Pursuing the Personal in Scholarship, Teaching, and Writing*, edited by James S. Baumlin and Keith D. Miller, NCTE, 2004, pp. 263–72.

———. "Argument as Emergence, Rhetoric as Love." *Rhetoric Review*, vol. 4, no. 1, Sept. 1985, pp. 16–32.

———. "From Rhetoric to Grace: Propositions 55–81 about Rhetoric, Propositions 1–54 and 82 et seq. Being as Yet Unstated, or Getting from the Classroom to the World." *Rhetoric Society Quarterly*, vol. 14.3, no. 4, 1984, pp. 15–28.

———. "I in Mine, You Elsewhere." *Selected Essays of Jim W. Corder: Pursuing the Personal in Scholarship, Teaching, and Writing*, edited by James S. Baumlin and Keith D. Miller, NCTE, 2004, pp. 243–62.

———. "On Cancer and Freshman Composition, or the Use of Rhetorical Language in the Description of Oncogenetic Behavior." *CEA Critic*, vol. 45, no. 1, 1982, pp. 1–9.

———. "Tribes and Displaced Persons: Some Observations on Collaboration." *Theory and Practice in the Teaching of Writing: Rethinking the Discipline*, edited by Lee O'Dell, Southern Illinois UP, 1993, pp. 271–88.

Crosby, Christina. *A Body, Undone: Living On after Great Pain*. New York UP, 2016.

Crowley, Sharon, and James Selzer, eds. *Rhetorical Bodies*. U of Wisconsin P, 1996.

Dadas, Caroline, Will Banks, and Matt Cox, eds. *Reorienting Writing Studies: Queer Methods, Queer Projects*. Utah State UP, forthcoming.

Daniell, Beth. *A Communion of Friendship: Literacy, Spiritual Practice, and Women in Recovery*. Southern Illinois UP, 2003.

Derrida, Jacques. *A Derrida Reader: Between the Blinds*, edited by Peggy Kamuf, Columbia UP, 1991.

DeVault, Marjorie L. *Liberating Method: Feminism and Social Research*. Temple UP, 1999.

DeVault, Marjorie, and Glenda Gross. "Feminist Interviewing: Experience, Talk, and Knowledge." *Handbook of Feminist Research*, 2nd ed., edited by Sharlene Nagy Hesse-Biber, Sage, 2012, pp. 173–97.

Dolmage, Jay. *Disability Rhetoric*. Syracuse UP, 2014.

Ede, Lisa. "Re: Feminisms and Rhetorics." Received by Jessica Restaino, 27 Oct. 2016.

———. "Re: She's gone." Received by Jessica Restaino, 29 Aug. 2014.

———. "Re: The latest." Received by Jessica Restaino, 24 July 2014.

Ede, Lisa, et al. "Border Crossings: Intersections of Rhetoric and Feminism." *Rhetorica: A Journal of the History of Rhetoric*, vol. 13, no. 4, Autumn 1995, pp. 401–41.

Ehrenreich, Barbara. *Bright-Sided: How the Relentless Promotion of Positive Thinking Has Undermined America*. Picador, 2010.

———. "Smile! You've Got Cancer." *The Guardian*, 1 Jan. 2010, www.theguardian.com/lifeandstyle/2010/jan/02/cancer-positive-thinking-barbara-ehrenreich. Accessed 17 Jan. 2017.

Eigen, Michael. *The Electrified Tightrope*. Jason Aronson, 1993.

Enos, Theresa, et al. *Beyond Postprocess and Postmodernism: Essays on the Spaciousness of Rhetoric*. Lawrence Erlbaum, 2003.

Ervin, Elizabeth. "Love Composes Us (in Memory of Jim Corder)." *Rhetoric Review*, vol. 17, no. 2, 1999, pp. 322–30.

———. "There's Nothing Good about Cancer." *Star News Online*, 28 Mar. 2008, www.starnewsonline.com/article/NC/20080328/news /605082441/WM/. Accessed 17 Jan. 2017

Evans, F. Barton. *Harry Stack Sullivan: Interpersonal Theory and Psychotherapy*. Routledge, 1996.

Faigley, Lester. "Literacy after the Revolution." *College Composition and Communication*, vol. 48, no. 1, 1997, pp. 30–43.

Fine, Michelle. "Working the Hyphens: Reinventing Self and Other in Qualitative Research." *The Landscape of Qualitative Research: Theories and Issues*, edited by Norman K. Denzin and Yvonna S. Lincoln. Sage, 1998, pp. 130–55.

Flax, Jane. *Thinking Fragments: Psychoanalysis, Feminism, and Postmodernism in the Contemporary West*. U of California P, 1990.

Foucault, Michel. *The History of Sexuality*. Pantheon Books, 1978.

Freud, Sigmund. "The Uncanny." *The Standard Edition of the Complete Psychological Works*, vol. 17, translated by James Strachey, Hogarth Press, 1955, p. 244.

Gere, Anne Ruggles. "Kitchen Tables and Rented Rooms: The Extracurriculum of College Composition." *College Composition and Communication*, vol. 45, 1994, pp. 75–91.

Ghent, Emmanuel. "Masochism, Submission, Surrender: Masochism as a Perversion of Surrender." *Contemporary Psychoanalysis*, vol. 26, no. 1, 1990, pp. 108–36.

Gilyard, Keith. *Voices of the Self: A Study of Language Competence*. Wayne State UP, 1991.

Glenn, Cheryl. *Unspoken: A Rhetoric of Silence*. Southern Illinois UP, 2004.

Gold, David. "Elizabeth Ervin and the Challenge of Civic Engagement: A Composition and Rhetoric Teacher's Struggle to Make Writing Matter." *Microhistories of Composition*, edited by Bruce McComisky, Utah State UP, 2016.

Goldblatt, Eli. "Don't Call It Expressivism: Legacies of a Tacit Tradition." *College Composition and Communication*, vol. 68, no. 3, 2017, pp. 438–65.

———. "Making Charoset: Teaching by Hand in the Shadow of MOOCS." *Another Word: From the Writing Center at the University of Wisconsin, Madison*, 1 Apr. 2013, writing.wisc.edu/blog/?p=3365. Accessed 17 Jan. 2017.

———. *'Round My Way: Authority and Double-Consciousness in Three Urban High School Writers*. U of Pittsburgh P, 1995.

Greene, Brian. "New Secrets of the Universe." *Newsweek*, 28 May 2012, pp. 23–25.

Halberstam, Jack. *The Queer Art of Failure*. Duke UP, 2011.

Harding, Sandra, ed. *The Feminist Standpoint Theory Reader: Intellectual and Political Controversies*. Routledge, 1994.

Hawhee, Debra. *Bodily Arts: Rhetoric and Athletics in Ancient Greece*. U of Texas P, 2004.

———. "Bodily Pedagogies: Rhetoric, Athletics, and the Sophists' Three Rs." *College English*, vol. 65, no. 2, Nov. 2002, pp. 142–62.

Hawke, Byron. *A Counter-History of Composition: Toward Methodologies of Complexity*. U of Pittsburgh P, 2007.

Herman, Judith Lewis. *Trauma and Recovery: The Aftermath of Violence—from Domestic Abuse to Political Terror*. Basic Books, 1997.

Homer. *The Iliad*. Translated by Alexander Pope, Create Space Publishing Platform, 2012.

"Houston, TX." *AVON 39: The Walk to End Breast Cancer*, www.avon39 .org/. Accessed 17 Jan. 2017.

Howard, Rebecca. "Embodiment, Machines, and the Posthuman." *Rebecca Moore Howard: Writing Matters*, www.rebeccamoorehoward.com /bibliographies/rhetorics-of-embodiment-and-the-posthuman. Accessed 17 Jan. 2017.

Hyland, Peter. *Shakespeare: Troilus and Cressida*. Penguin Books, 1989.

Jung, C. G. *Synchronicity: An Acausal Connecting Principle*. Princeton UP, 1973.

Kerschbaum, Stephanie. *Toward a New Rhetoric of Difference*. Southern Illinois UP, 2014.

Kirsch, Gesa. "Friendship, Friendliness, and Feminist Fieldwork." *Signs*, vol. 30, no. 4, Summer 2005, pp. 2163–72.

Kirsch, Gesa, and Liz Rohan, eds. *Beyond the Archives: Research as a Lived Process*. Southern Illinois UP, 2008.

Kirsch, Gesa, and Jacqueline Jones Royster. *Feminist Rhetorical Practices: New Horizons for Rhetoric, Composition, and Literacy Studies*. Southern Illinois UP, 2012.

Kübler-Ross, Elisabeth. *On Death and Dying*. Macmillan, 1969.

Lather, Patti. "Postbook: Troubling the Ruins of Feminist Ethnography." *Signs*, vol. 27, no. 1, Autumn 2000, pp. 199–227.

Lather, Patti, and Chris Smithies. *Troubling the Angels: Women Living with HIV/AIDS*. Westview Press, 1997.

Levi, Albert William. "Love, Rhetoric, and the Aristocratic Way of Life." *Philosophy and Rhetoric*, vol. 17, no. 4, 1 Jan. 1984, pp. 189–208.

Lorde, Audre. *The Cancer Journals*. Aunt Lute Books, 1997.

Loy, Mina. "Parturition." *The Lost Lunar Baedecker: Poems of Mina Loy*, edited by Roger L. Conover, Farrar, Straus, and Giroux, 1997, pp. 4–8.

Lunsford, Andrea A., and Lisa S. Ede. *Writing Together: Collaboration in Theory and Practice, a Critical Sourcebook*. Bedford/St. Martins, 2012.

Mattingly, Cheryl, and Linda C. Garro. *Narrative and the Cultural Construction of Illness and Healing*. U of California P, 2000.

Maute, Susan Lundy. "Class visit writing." 12 June 2012. Unpub.

———. "Hello Cancer." Sept. 2013.

———. Personal interview. 31 May 2013.

———. Personal interview. 20 June 2013.

———. Personal interview. 24 Mar. 2014.

———. Personal interview (handwritten notes). 14 Apr. 2014.

———. Personal interview. 2 May 2014.

———. "Project Purpose Response." 16 Aug. 2013. Unpub.

———. "Re: And thank you" (text message). Received by Jessica Restaino, 9 July 2014.

———. "Re: Direction." Received by Jessica Restaino, 23 June 2013.

———. "Re: Essay Feedback." Received by Jessica Restaino, 5 Oct. 2013.

———. "Re: Gratitude." Received by Jessica Restaino, 20 Mar. 2014.

———. "Re: Heading to hospital." Received by Jessica Restaino, 8 July 2014.

———. "Re: I Love You" (text message). Received by Jessica Restaino, 12 July 2014.

———. "Re: Interesting morning" (text message). Received by Jessica Restaino, 9 July 2014.

———. "Re: O wise literary one" (text message). Received by Jessica Restaino, 19 July 2014.

———. "Rough Times July 2013." 9 July 2013. Unpub.

———. "What I Want." 8 Aug. 2014. Unpub.

"Mayo Clinic." *Mayo Clinic*, www.mayoclinic.org/. Accessed 17 Jan. 2017.

Mazzei, Lisa A. *Inhabited Silence in Qualitative Research: Putting Poststructural Theory to Work*. Peter Lang, 2007.

———. "Silent Listenings: Deconstructive Practices in Discourse-Based Research." *Educational Researcher*, vol. 33, no. 2, Mar. 2004, pp. 26–34.

McKee, Heidi, and James Porter. "The Ethics of Archival Research." *College Composition and Communication*, vol. 64, no. 1, 2012, pp. 59–81.

Miller, Richard. "The Nervous System." *College English*, vol. 58, no. 3, Mar. 1996, pp. 265–86.

Miller, Susan. *Textual Carnivals: The Politics of Composition.* Southern Illinois UP, 1991.

Narang, Amol, et al. "Trends in Advance Care Planning in Patients with Cancer." *JAMA Oncology*, vol. 1, no. 5, 2015, pp. 601–8.

Newkirk, Thomas. *Minds Made for Stories: How We Really Read and Write Informational and Persuasive Texts.* Heinemann, 2014.

———. "Seduction and Betrayal in Qualitative Research." *Ethics and Representation in Qualitative Studies of Literacy*, edited by Peter Mortensen and Gesa Kirsch, NCTE, 1996, pp. 3–16.

Newkirk, Thomas, and Lad Tobin. "Personal Writing." Conference on College Composition and Communication, Mar. 2015, Tampa, FL.

Noddings, Nel. *Caring, a Feminine Approach to Ethics and Moral Education.* U of California P, 1984.

Orenstein, Peggy. "Our Feel-Good War on Breast Cancer." *New York Times Magazine*, 25 Apr. 2013.

———. "The Wrong Approach to Breast Cancer." *New York Times*, 26 July 2014.

The Oxford English Dictionary. 2nd ed. Edited by John A. Simpson. Clarendon Press, 1989.

Peck, M. Scott. *The Road Less Traveled: A New Psychology of Love, Traditional Values, and Spiritual Growth.* Simon and Schuster, 1978.

Perl, Sondra. *On Austrian Soil: Teaching Those I Was Taught to Hate.* State U of New York P, 2005.

Ratcliffe, Krista. *Rhetorical Listening: Identification, Gender, Whiteness.* Southern Illinois UP, 2005.

Rawlins, William K. *The Compass of Friendship: Narratives, Identities, and Dialogues.* Sage, 2009.

Restaino, Jessica. "Notes on Sue's Goal, 25 September 2013." Unpub.

———. "Performing Feminist Action: A Toolbox for Feminist Research and Teaching." *Peitho: Journal of the Coalition of Feminist Scholars in the History of Rhetoric and Composition*, cwshrc.org/blog/2015/04/12/actionhour/. Accessed 17 Jan. 2017.

———. "Project Purpose Response." 16 Aug. 2013. Unpub.

———. "Re: Direction." Received by Susan Lundy Maute, 20 June 2013.

———. "Reflection: Alternate Orbit." 26 March. 2014. Unpub.

———. "Reflection: Athlete." 11 Mar. 2014. Unpub.

———. "Reflection: Hair." 18 Feb. 2014. Unpub.

———. "Reflection: Hospice." 17 Sept. 2014. Unpub.

———. "Reflection: Walk to Lake." 2 Aug. 2014. Unpub.

———. "Reflection: Week of 7/7/14." 7 July 2014. Unpub.

———. "Re: Rode the Light" (text message). Received by Susan Lundy Maute, 10 Aug. 2014.

———. "Re: She's gone." Received by Lisa Ede, 29 Aug. 2014.

———. "Re: Small Update." Received by Lisa Ede, 9 July 2014.

———. "Saturday Night at Morristown Memorial, 9 August 2015." Unpub.

———. "Syllabus: ENWR 220: Rhetoric of Sport." Summer 2012, Montclair State U. Unpub.

Restaino, Jessica, and Susan Lundy Maute. "No Evidence of Disease: Research, Collaboration, Expectation, and Feminist Practice." Feminisms and Rhetorics Conference, Oct. 2013, Palo Alto, Stanford U.

———. "Surrender as Method: Research, Writing, Rhetoric, Love." *Peitho: Journal of the Coalition of Feminist Scholars in the History of Rhetoric and Composition*, vol. 18, no. 1, Fall/Winter 2015, peitho.cwshrc.org /issue/18-1/. Accessed 17 Jan. 2017.

Rhodes, Jacqueline. *Radical Feminism, Writing, and Critical Agency: From Manifesto to Modem.* State U of New York P, 2005.

———. "Rhizomes." *Techne: Queer Meditations on Writing the Self,* by Jacqueline Rhodes and Jonathan Alexander, Computers and Composition Digital Press, ccdigitalpress.org/ebooks-and-projects/techne. Accessed 17 Jan. 2017.

———. "Susan Miller and the Queer Subject of Composition." Conference on College Composition and Communication, Apr. 2016, Houston, TX.

Rhodes, Jacqueline, and Jonathan Alexander. *Techne: Queer Meditations on Writing the Self,* Computers and Composition Digital Press, ccdigital press.org/ebooks-and-projects/techne. Accessed 17 Jan. 2017.

Rich, Adrienne. "When We Dead Awaken: Writing as Re-vision." *College English*, vol. 34, no. 1, Oct. 1972, pp. 18–30.

Richard Feynman: The Pleasure of Finding Things Out. Produced by Christopher Sykes, BBC, 1981.

Rickly, Rebecca. "Messy Contexts: Research as a Rhetorical Situation." *Digital Writing Research: Technologies, Methodologies, and Ethical Issues,* edited by Heidi A. McKee and Nicole DeVoss, Hampton Press, 2007, pp. 377–97.

Roberts-Miller, Patricia. *Deliberate Conflict: Argument, Political Theory, and Composition Classes.* Southern Illinois UP, 2004.

Rose, Mike. *Lives on the Boundary: The Struggles and Achievements of America's Underprepared.* Free Press, 1989.

———. *Writer's Block: The Cognitive Dimension.* Southern Illinois UP, 2009.

Roskelly, Hephzibah, and Kate Ronald. *Reason to Believe: Romanticism, Pragmatism, and the Teaching of Writing.* State U of New York P, 1998.

Rushdie, Salman. "February 1999: Ten Years after the Fatwa." *Step across This Line: Collected Non-fiction, 1992–2002.* Jonathan Cape, 2002, p. 294.

Schell, Eileen, and Ivy Kleinbart. "'I Have to Speak Out': Writing with Veterans in a Community Writing Group." *Generation Vet: Composition, Student Veterans, and the Post-9/11 University*, edited by Susan Doe and Lisa Lanstraat, U of Colorado P, 2014, pp. 119–39.

Schell, Eileen E., and K. J. Rawson. *Rhetorica in Motion: Feminist Rhetorical Methods and Methodologies.* U of Pittsburgh P, 2010.

Schell, Eileen E., and Patricia L. Stock. *Moving a Mountain: Transforming the Role of Contingent Faculty in Composition Studies and Higher Education.* NCTE, 2001.

"The Secret in the Cellar." *Written in Bone—The Secret in the Cellar: A Written in Bone Forensic Mystery from Colonial America*, anthropology. si.edu/writteninbone/comic/. Accessed 17 Jan. 2017.

Shakespeare, William. *Troilus and Cressida: The Oxford Shakespeare.* Oxford UP, 2008.

Shipka, Jody. "To Gather, Assemble and Display: Composition as (re) Collection." *Assembling Composition*, edited by Kathleen Blake Yancey and Stephen McElroy, NCTE, 2017, pp. 143–60.

Smagorinsky, Peter. "The Method Section as Conceptual Epicenter in Constructing Social Science Research Reports." *Written Communication*, vol. 25, no. 3, 2008, pp. 389–412.

———. "Transparency in Research: Messiness, Rigor, and Ethics in the Conduct of Writing Research." Conference on College Composition and Communication, Mar. 2015, Tampa, FL.

Søndergaard, Dorte Marie. "Angels and Research: Review of *Troubling the Angels*." *Educational Researcher*, Oct. 2000, pp. 31–33.

Sontag, Susan. *Illness as Metaphor.* Farrar, Straus and Giroux, 1978.

Spivak, Gayatri Chakravorty, et al. *The Spivak Reader: Selected Works of Gayatri Chakravorty Spivak.* Routledge, 1996.

Sullivan, Patricia. "Ethnography and the Problem of the 'Other.'" *Ethics and Representation in Qualitative Studies of Literacy*, edited by Peter Mortensen and Gesa Kirsch, NCTE, 1996, pp. 97–119.

"Susan G. Komen®." *Susan G. Komen*, ww5.komen.org/. Accessed 17 Jan. 2017.

Swarts, Jason. "Collecting, Analyzing, and Talking about Data." Conference on College Composition and Communication, Mar. 2014, Indianapolis, IN.

"Syracuse Veterans' Writing Group." *WRT: Syracuse Veterans' Writing Group Writing Program: Arts and Sciences: Syracuse University*, wrt. syr.edu/syrvetwriters/. Accessed 17 Jan. 2017.

Tobin, Lad. *Reading Student Writing: Confessions, Meditations, and Rants.* Boynton/Cook/Heinemann, 2004.

———. "Telling the Tales in and out of School: Beyond the Binary of Personal vs. Scholarly Writing." Conference on College Composition and Communication, Mar. 2015, Tampa, FL.

"The Top 20 Things Oprah Knows for Sure." *Oprah.com*, www.oprah. com/spirit/The-Top-20-Things-Oprah-Knows-for-Sure. Accessed 17 Jan. 2017.

Van der Kolk, Bessel A. *The Body Keeps the Score: Brain, Mind, and Body in the Healing of Trauma.* Viking, 2014.

Van Manen, Max. "The Pathic Nature of Inquiry and Nursing." *Nursing and the Experience of Illness: Phenomenology in Practice*, Routledge, 1999, pp. 17–35.

Villanueva, Victor. *Bootstraps: From an American Academic of Color.* NCTE, 1993.

Virgil. *The Georgics.* Translated by John Dryden, Heritage Press, 1953.

Walters, Shannon. *Rhetorical Touch: Disability, Identification, Haptics.* U of South Carolina P, 2014.

Wells, Susan. *Our Bodies, Ourselves and the Work of Writing.* Stanford UP, 2010.

Young, Stella. "I'm Not Your Inspiration, Thank You Very Much." *TED: Ideas Worth Spreading*, Apr. 2014, www.ted.com/talks/stella_young _i_m_not_your_inspiration_thank_you_very_much. Accessed 17 Jan. 2017.

INDEX

Jessica Restaino is Associate Professor of Writing Studies and Director of Gender, Sexuality, and Women's Studies at Montclair State University. She is the author of *First Semester: Graduate Students, Teaching Writing, and the Challenge of Middle Ground* and a coeditor, with Laurie Cella, of *Unsustainable: Re-imagining Community Literacy, Public Writing, Service-Learning, and the University.*